"*Yoga and the Pursuit of Happiness* weaves together philosophy, centuries-old yoga tools, and the modern day sciences of psychology and neurobiology with incredible readability. It takes years of study, lots of deep thinking, and plenty of practice to untangle key threads and weave them together in in such a completely accessible, thorough, and totally relevant way. This is a must-read for all yoga practitioners—and anyone who wants to cultivate more happiness."

—**Megan McDonough**, CEO of Wholebeing Institute, and
author of *Infinity in a Box* and *Radically Receptive Meditation*

"This is one of those rare books that can change your life for the better. By bridging yoga and psychology, philosophical discourse and practical tips, and personal stories and rigorous research, Sam Chase takes us on a journey of self-discovery and self-transformation."

—**Tal Ben-Shahar, PhD**, best-selling author of *Happier* and
Choose the Life You Want

"In this book, Sam Chase manages to explain deep and complex questions that cut to the core of the human mind, heart, and body with the easy and intimate tone of good friends having a conversation over tea. I laughed out loud. I reached for my pen to underline sentences. I didn't want to stop reading. The book is filled with so much wisdom, depth, humor, and compassion. Chase takes us on a journey to happiness that begins with an inability to touch his toes and ends with an understanding of ourselves as more vast and precious than we could possibly imagine."

—**Yael Shy**, senior director of Global Spiritual Life at New York
University, and founder and director of MindfulNYU

"Weaving together ideas from various traditions—including yoga, Buddhism, and positive psychology—Sam Chase gives his readers an enjoyable manual for developing happiness. *Yoga and the Pursuit of Happiness* contains no pictures or postures, just sound guidance on how to reconnect with your innate joyfulness."

—**Sharon Salzberg**, author of *Lovingkindness* and *Real Happiness*

"*Yoga and the Pursuit of Happiness* is a comprehensive book that presents the traditional goals of yoga as they are understood by modern neuroscience and positive psychology. Certainly, this is not a book about how to perform yoga poses. Sam Chase offers a heartfelt and genuine account of his *discovery* of yoga. With numerous personal anecdotes and scientific evidence—many of them written with candor and a great sense of humor—Sam advises us to take yoga as an exploration, and tells us that with open eyes and curiosity we can discover many things that we had not noticed before. From the opening pages, Chase affirms that the ultimate goal of yoga is to achieve happiness. This is a recommended book for all yoga practitioners and curious minds who would like to know and explore the true meaning of yoga."

—**Germán A. Bravo-Casas**, president of the Yoga Club
at the United Nations (UNSRC)

"Sam Chase's new book is a delightful and extremely informative examination of the practical genius of yoga. Chase has a particularly good eye for storytelling and illuminating scientific discovery, and he weaves these together in such a compelling way that I guarantee that you won't want to put this book down! Yoga students—beginners as well as advanced—will be very glad, indeed, to have this new book."

—**Stephen Cope**, senior scholar in residence at the Kripalu
Center for Yoga and Health, and author of the best-selling
Yoga and the Quest for the True Self

YOGA

& the PURSUIT of HAPPINESS

A Beginner's Guide to Finding Joy in Unexpected Places

SAM CHASE

New Harbinger Publications, Inc.

Publisher's Note

"The VIA Classification of Character Strengths and Values" in chapter 6 is © copyright 2004–2014, VIA Institute on Character. Used with permission; all rights reserved. http://www.viacharacter.org.

Distributed in Canada by Raincoast Books

Copyright © 2016 by Sam Chase
    New Harbinger Publications, Inc.
    5674 Shattuck Avenue
    Oakland, CA 94609
    www.newharbinger.com

Cover design by Sara Christian

Acquired by Melissa Kirk

Edited by Marisa Solís

All Rights Reserved

Library of Congress Cataloging-in-Publication Data on file

Printed in the United States of America

18   17   16

10   9   8   7   6   5   4   3   2   1   First printing

Contents

Introduction

I started yoga because I wanted to be able to touch my toes. I had no higher aspirations at the time. Growing up severely asthmatic and comically unathletic, I finished the mile run during elementary school gym class dead last in 15 minutes, then promptly threw up. My body and I were not on what you would call "speaking terms." I regarded it as a constantly malfunctioning annoyance, and it routinely lived up to the low expectation I set.

I knew a losing bet even as a grade-schooler, and quickly swapped physical pursuits for intellectual ones. For a while it seemed like I'd struck quite a deal on the trade: I graduated as valedictorian of my high school class, then of my college class as well. My mind was clearly succeeding where my body had failed, so "Good riddance," I thought.

And that's when things started to fall apart. At the end of college, I was invited to apply to a scholarship program to study in England, one of the most prestigious in my field at the time, with only a handful awarded among thousands of applicants around the country. I have a vivid memory of getting the congratulatory call that ought to have elated me. For a young academic, there was no higher pinnacle, and I was standing at the top. It was supposed to be the best moment of my life. Instead, panic flooded in where joy should have been setting sail, and the familiar wheeze of vanishing breath returned. And then I threw up.

With that, my old nemesis—my body—began its most brilliant betrayal. I tried desperately to will myself to enjoy the sudden success, but something in me refused. And whatever it was, it dug its heels in deep. In the days that followed, each congratulatory pat on the back felt like a punch in the guts. Every time I thought of the door to my future, now standing wide open, I broke out in a cold sweat.

I knew, even then, that I was agonizing over an incredibly privileged problem, a fact that made the wound even saltier. But every time I tried to jump at the opportunity of a lifetime, something held me down at the ankles. After a week of self-flagellating deliberation, I said no to the scholarship. Friends and professors called me a fool. I agreed. I had no backup plan, no brighter future in mind. The awkward breathlessness of my youth began to blossom into an adulthood of apathy and anxiety.

Months later, I ended a romantic relationship of several years, again, without knowing exactly why. Again, with my brain screaming, "What the hell are you doing?!" while something strange inside carried on demolishing the life I had so carefully manufactured. But there was no poltergeist to point to. It was a mess entirely of my own making, and the fact that I couldn't find any rational reason for my behavior just compounded my sense of shame. Over the ensuing year, depression moved in so gradually that I can't say when it arrived. It redecorated day by day with little touches, until it seemed as though we had always been living together this way.

My life flatlined like this until, in a rare spasm of determination, I decided to resuscitate my happiness by learning to touch my toes. I recalled an annual ritual from that same grade-school gym class called the President's Fitness Challenge, a grim spectacle involving all kinds of exercises tailor-made to renew my conviction that my body would still not be doing me any favors. The particular torture that stuck in my mind most was the "sit and reach," whereby you sit straight legged on the floor, fold forward, and stretch your fingers as far past your toes as possible. A ruler measures your success from zero to presumably infinity. In my case, unable to reach even to my socks, another ruler going in the other direction recorded my utter lack of flexibility. Amid a sea of elastic children scoring nines and tens and one shocking rubber band of a sixteen, I hid my minus four and awaited the letter I would surely receive from the President informing me that I had failed his Challenge and disappointed my country.

From the low vantage of depression, touching my toes was just about the only feeble gasp of purpose I could muster. Yoga, or what little I knew of it, seemed like a good enough place to start. If my self-esteem hadn't already lost hold and hit rock bottom, that first class probably would have stomped on my grip until I plummeted. My toes were farther away than ever; the minus four of my childhood had become a sobering minus eight. Every strange pose I was introduced to seemed to call up body parts I had broken up with long ago, and they all answered the phone angry. Finally, the class lay down for something called *savasana*, which was, near as I could tell, a nap by another name. I was pretty sure I hated everything about yoga.

When I sat up after the nap, nothing happened. I mean that literally: my body wasn't hurting, my mind wasn't racing, I wasn't wondering what the heck I was going to do with my life, and, for just a few seconds, *nothing happened*. I wasn't happy. I wasn't sad. I just *was*. There was a sharpness, a vividness to everything—and a sense of deep stillness so foreign to my usual way of being that it came as a jolt. It left just as abruptly, and the familiar unease nestled right back into its favorite spot in the pit of my stomach. But, for that little moment when nothing happened, I kept going back.

In a few weeks I could touch my toes. In a few months I put away my inhaler and have scarcely used it since. Bit by bit, the anxiety that had me cornered in my own life backed off. One evening much later that year, hurrying out of the subway, I caught the sunset glancing off the windows of an office tower at a particularly stunning angle and paused. A moment of bright, still nothingness for which I had no other name washed over me again and left in its wake a sense of quiet bliss. I almost discarded the moment unnoticed, like a love letter tucked into a stack of junk mail. Happiness had snuck back into my psyche when I was scarcely looking. And I had been looking long and hard.

Seeking Stillness

This is not an extraordinary story of yoga. It is a story of yoga doing exactly what yoga is designed to do: illuminate a stillness at the heart of each and every one of us that cannot be threatened by time or circumstance. Like a word you hear for the first time and then suddenly start encountering everywhere, if you go out seeking this kind of stillness, you will hear it spoken about in nearly every corner of the world. Ancient Chinese philosopher Lao-tzu said, "To the mind that is still, the whole universe surrenders." Medieval Christian mystic Meister Eckhart wrote, "Nothing in all creation is so like God as stillness." To my mind, twentieth-century author Franz Kafka captured it best:

You do not need to leave your room. Remain sitting at your table and listen. Do not even listen, simply wait, be quiet, still and solitary. The world will freely offer itself to you to be unmasked, it has no choice, it will roll in ecstasy at your feet. (2012, 188)

The ecstasy at our feet that Kafka describes is not for the philosophers and mystics alone. In recent years, psychologists and neuroscientists have turned their inquiries toward stillness and bliss, and in doing so they have begun to discover how yoga's deeper practices like meditation change our minds, rewire our brains, and touch every cell of our bodies.

This book is a conversation at the crossroads where the philosophy and contemplative practices of yoga and Buddhism meet up with the disciplines of psychology and neuroscience to talk about what makes us happy. Often they find surprising common ground that crosses oceans and millennia. Just as often they argue, sometimes over the most simple-seeming ideas—such as what "happiness" means and who the "I" in "I am happy" really is. We take these topics for granted on a daily basis; you have felt happy, hopefully many times over, and each time it feels like there's a "you" that happiness is happening to. But if we pause to delve into the nature of happiness and the substance of the self, all of these traditions reveal a vast frontier beneath our everyday thoughts awaiting exploration.

This is a book for those with a yearning to reach further into self-understanding, whether or not you ever dare to touch your toes. Beneath the postures that have become so prevalent in modern yoga lies a rich philosophy rooted in the quest to understand who we really are, and a set of tools designed for self-transformation. Those tools take the form of meditation, which has its roots in Indian philosophical systems dating back thousands of years but has been best preserved and popularized in Buddhist contemplative practices that we'll explore throughout this book. Along the way, we'll thread these ancient philosophies and practices together with fascinating findings from modern psychology and neuroscience about our nature and our potential to shape our own happiness.

This book draws particularly on a branch of psychology designed around the study of human flourishing called *positive psychology*. Positive psychology was a field I literally snuck into. While I attended Harvard, a class on happiness taught by Tal Ben-Shahar made national headlines as the university's most popular course, enrolling more than eight hundred students. Curious about the hubbub and certain that an extra inquiring mind wouldn't be noticed, I regularly crashed his positive psychology class and lurked in the back of the room, even though I belonged to an entirely different department. Nearly a decade later, Tal and I crossed paths again in the Berkshires, at the Kripalu Center for Yoga and Health, the nation's largest yoga center, where I had become a faculty member in the yoga program and where he had developed the center's Positive Psychology certificate program. This time around, I enrolled properly and sat in front. The insights of positive psychology share center stage with yoga and meditation throughout this book.

Inquire Within

Each chapter of this book contains several exercises and experiences designed to put the ideas we'll be exploring into practice. They're called Inquiries. Do them. There's a reason yoga and meditation are referred to as "practice" and not as "just sit there and read about it." What you discover along this ride into the self will result from what you do along the way, not from what you read. Mythologist Joseph Campbell eloquently champions the necessity of having a space for practice in our lives:

> You must have a room, or a certain hour or so a day, where you don't know what was in the newspapers that morning, you don't know who your friends are, you don't know what you owe anybody, you don't know what anybody owed to you. This is a place where you can simply experience and bring forth what you are and what you might be. This is the place of creative incubation. At first you may find that nothing happens there. But if you have a sacred place and use it, something eventually will happen. (1991, 115)

Yoga, meditation, and science share this dedication to practice. In science, theories alone are worthless unless they stand up to experimentation. The Inquiries throughout this book are opportunities not only to develop an understanding of how your happiness ticks but also to make a laboratory of your own life and to experiment with your everyday experiences. At first you may feel like nothing happens, but if you follow the practices throughout the book, you will see your self differently on the other side. So get ready, because you've got an Inquiry coming up in just a few pages.

Ultimately, this is not a manual on how to be happy. It's a mistake to suppose that simply practicing yoga or dabbling in neuropsychology will lead anyone to happiness. Yoga did not make me happy—but it did give me a space in which I could study myself and the sources of my happiness, as well as the tools to take those insights off the mat and transform daily life. This book will not tell you what to craft with these tools, but it will teach you how to hold them. Science can't tell you what to change in you, but it will help you understand the nature of change and how to make it stick. This book will not tell you what happiness to pursue, but it can help you pack for the journey.

The Bhagavad Gita and The Yoga Sutras

This book relies on two central texts from the yoga tradition: the Bhagavad Gita and *The Yoga Sutras*. Both were originally written in Sanskrit, a ritual language that's several thousand years old. I'm not a Sanskrit scholar; I half-jokingly tell people that I know enough Sanskrit to get myself into trouble but not enough to get out of trouble. Since I started exploring yoga, my own understanding of the Gita and the *Sutras* has been illuminated by teachers and translators too numerous to mention here, and I am unendingly grateful to the many voices that have interpreted these works for hundreds of years.

Nonetheless, in this book I've chosen to translate quotations from the Gita and the *Sutras* myself. Yoga philosophy frequently shares terms with psychology and neuroscience, but it often uses the same term to point toward a very different concept. So, in translation, I've endeavored to keep the conversation clear, consistent, and—I believe—faithful to the originals. But you don't have to take my word for it: with each quote I've included chapter and line numbers so you can see how other writers have interpreted these challenging texts.

The Gita and the *Sutras* have roots in India's Hindu religions, yet both have endured to become today's most popular treatises on yoga philosophy for people of myriad faiths. Hinduism encompasses an incredibly diverse set of spiritual and wisdom traditions—among the oldest on record in the world—with complicated and often conflicting conversations about the nature and existence of divinity. The Gita in particular has been used throughout history to craft a philosophy of yoga for religious as well as secular goals.

This book is concerned with two main questions: "What's up with this thing called the self?" and "How can I make my self happier?" I'll just be frank in saying that if we were to throw in the question "So what about God?" this book would be way too long, and I wouldn't presume to know how to answer that question. Gandhi described the Gita as "a work which persons belonging to all faiths can read. It does not favor any sectarian point of view. It teaches nothing but pure ethics" (2000, 205). Throughout this book, we'll follow Gandhi's lead and explore these essential works of yoga from a largely secular standpoint.

PART I

THE MAP

CHAPTER 1

The Pursuit of Happiness

There are three Things extremely hard: Steel, a Diamond,
and to know one's Self.

—Benjamin Franklin, statesman and scientist

The first thing I want you to do is put this book down. I am told by many
published authors that this is a horrible sentence to start a book with, but
I have to be up-front: you're about to hear from a whole bunch of philosophers and scientists about what they think happiness is. Before your head
gets crowded with a lot of notions from dead guys and nerds (and dead
nerd guys), put this book down, grab a pen, and write for a few minutes
about what *you* think happiness is.

If you're still holding the book thinking, "Whatever, I'll do that later.
You wrote a whole book, so why don't *you* just tell me what happiness is,
smart guy," then I am now writing specifically to you. Yes, you: *do it*. Once
someone else's ideas start crawling around in your brain, it's really hard to
get them out. It'll be nice at the end to have a little memento of what you
thought way back here at the beginning. If you did it, great, then carry
on... If not, well, don't say I didn't warn you: the whole book is full of
Inquiries like this, and sooner or later you'll have to make it personal.

The Why of Happiness

I meet people trying yoga for the first time every single day, and I always
ask the same question: "Why are you doing yoga?" I have heard hundreds

of answers: to shape up or slim down or be more flexible or focused or, my personal favorite, "I need to survive Thanksgiving without strangling my parents." Never once in years of offering classes have I heard someone say, "I don't know." The reason could be big or small, buried deep or sitting right on the surface, but I believe you don't step onto a yoga mat unless you want something in your life to change.

As different as all those desires look from the outside, if we dig in a little to ask, "Why? Why do I want that?" eventually we're going to hit happiness. Tal Ben-Shahar, the teacher I met at Harvard and Kripalu, refers to this as "the infinitely regressive why" (2007). I want to do yoga so I am calm. Why? So I don't throttle my family. Why? So we love each other. Why? Because a loving family makes me happy. But why do I want to be happy?

Happiness is the "Why?" that won't budge, though great minds have been pushing on it for millennia. From ancient Greece, Aristotle concluded, "Happiness is the meaning and the purpose of life, the whole aim and end of human existence." It is a bedrock human emotion, and once we hit upon it, no more asking why will dig us any deeper. With some finality, thirteenth-century Christian philosopher Thomas Aquinas dubbed happiness "man's last end." More recently, the Dalai Lama eloquently summarized the Buddhist perspective on our inescapable arrival at the question of happiness:

> One great question underlies our experience, whether we think about it consciously or not: What is the purpose of life?... I believe that the purpose of life is to be happy. From the moment of birth, every human being wants happiness and does not want suffering... I don't know whether the universe, with its countless galaxies, stars and planets, has a deeper meaning or not, but at the very least, it is clear that we humans who live on this earth face the task of making a happy life for ourselves. (2011, 2)

A happy life comes with a lot of perks. Happy people live longer and have better immune function. They make more money and are more likeable. They are more optimistic and resilient. That's a pretty sweet deal for happy folks, but it's also good for everyone around them, too. Happy people are more politically and civically active. They are more productive at work and express more creativity in problem solving. Happy people have stronger marriages as well as more and closer friendships. They are also more philanthropic and more altruistic. While it's tough to determine whether happiness causes these things, or the other way around, they are all significant correlations (Lyubomirsky, King, and Diener 2005). Of course, there's one thing happiness causes that you don't need any research to understand: it makes us feel pretty darn great.

Happiness seems to speak for itself, and the pursuit of happiness permeates everything we do. Whether reaching for our toes or searching for enlightenment, each of us is, one way or another, in the pursuit of happiness. If that's the case, it will help to know a bit about what we're aiming for.

Inquiry: The Infinitely Regressive "Why?"

Take a minute to write down things you desire—as many as come to mind. They can be goals, objects, emotions, or anything at all. Try not to evaluate or analyze for the moment, and don't worry whether they make sense or not right now. Just allow your thoughts to emerge and record them as they come.

Pick three desires that stick out to you today, and start to trace them backward. Why do you want that? And why do you want *that*? Notice where your inquiry leads you. Are there common threads within your desires? Do they arrive in similar places?

Three Happinesses

Once we have drilled down to the bedrock of happiness with the question "Why?" other questions spring right up. "How do I really know I'm happy? What *is* happiness anyhow?" The last of these is my particular favorite. If you ever want to ruin a perfectly good conversation at a party, try asking people what they believe happiness is and watch them start to squirm.

Asking someone to define happiness is like asking if they've gotten that mole looked at: we know we should get it sorted out, but we're all very busy and a little nervous about what'll happen if we do, and bringing it up in company is just rude.

Philosophers, however, love to talk about the nature of happiness at parties, which is why they are never invited. Yet for all their consensus on the pivotal role of happiness in life, the trio of philosophers we met earlier can scarcely agree on what it is. Aristotle's word for happiness was *eudaemonia*, which literally means "good spirit" and is often translated as living well in accordance with virtues. He described *eudaemonia* as a behavior rather than a state of being—not something you feel but something you do by expressing humanity's highest faculties in action. As a Christian, Aquinas found the happiness of "man's last end" in the contemplative experience of God, which could be realized fully only in the afterlife. The Dalai Lama focuses his Buddhist understanding of happiness on the cultivation of self-transcending compassion and altruism in the here and now.

Each of these three captures a robust but distinct philosophy of happiness: Aristotle argues for an active expression of one's skill and morality in the world, Aquinas focuses on a connection with divinity that transcends this world, and the Dalai Lama encourages self-transcendence, too, but with a more earthbound focus on compassion for others. The subtle tensions between the happiness each describes raises key questions: Where should I look for happiness? To myself? To others? To divinity?

If we were to toss a few more philosophers into the mix, the conversation would get rowdy pretty quickly. So if your own answer to the question "What is happiness?" still feels a bit murky, you're in good company. For now, we might dodge the challenge with a page from the playbook of Supreme Court Justice Potter Stewart, who was pressed to define obscenity in court and replied famously, "I know it when I see it." Maybe we just know happiness when we feel it. Or do we?

If You're Happy and You Know It...

If you've ever sat through lunch with gritted teeth while a friend gushes over how she's "*soooooo* happy" with her latest mismatched romantic fling, you know that your happiness and that of the person sitting across from you sometimes don't look anything alike. If we're all just sailing toward bliss on our own private ships, some people are on the *Titanic* and don't seem to know it. But if we're so sure our lunch buddy has no clue how unhappy she is, do we really even know how happy we are?

This is one of the central questions of an emerging science called positive psychology, formally founded by Martin Seligman in 1998 and dedicated to studying the content and causes of happiness and human flourishing. While psychology plied the tools of scientific inquiry on the sources of our displeasure and despair for well over a century, for the most part it left the philosophers and poets to hash out happiness. If it can't be measured, scientists generally want nothing to do with it, and the radical subjectivity of happiness seemed to place it well beyond the reach of empiricism's gold standard: the randomized controlled study. But intrepid researchers forged on nonetheless and discovered that the same tools and methods that help us understand how things go wrong with the human mind can also shed some surprising light on how things go right.

While it's tricky to determine much about how one individual's experience of happiness stacks up against another's, when we stack up lots and lots of people, these little quirks disappear. Large-group comparisons using numerous simple scales have shown that, in fact, self-reported assessments of our own happiness are usually quite reliable (Lyubomirsky and Lepper 1999; Krueger and Schkade 2008). Further research using fMRI and PET scans to measure brain activity found a significant response in an area known as the left prefrontal cortex when subjects were experiencing happiness (Davidson 2004). It took a $1 million measuring stick to do it, but researchers were able to map *where* in the brain our happiness happens and show that it was remarkably consistent from person to person.

Let's not forget that for all the expensive equipment, the whole process ultimately boils down to a researcher watching a picture of your brain light up on the screen and asking, "Now! What are you feeling *right now?*" Beyond the graphs and gizmos, the science of happiness is still built on the bedrock of listening to what you say about what you feel. Consider the alternative: you walk into a lab feeling horribly depressed, lie down in an fMRI tube, and a researcher with a very furrowed brow says, "Well, I understand you say you're feeling miserable, but your left prefrontal cortex is lighting up like crazy. I'm sorry to say you're actually extremely happy." This makes no sense. If you can be happy and not know it, then happiness becomes something outside of your conscious experience, a state that exists independently of whether you are aware enough to notice or not. Once we remove awareness from the picture, statements about happiness start to become nonsense. As Harvard psychologist Daniel Gilbert points out, it doesn't make much sense to say something like, "Sue was happy to be in a coma," because the very notion of happiness rests on the fact that there is an awareness named Sue in the unique position to experience that emotion (2006). Once the awareness is gone, as is the case with a coma, the experiencer of happiness vanishes. There's no *there* there.

How WEIRD Are You?

While this book frequently draws on rigorous research, it's important to acknowledge that scientific studies are not flawless. One study of the top psychology journals indicated that roughly 95 percent of psychological research relied on people from Western, educated, industrialized, rich, and democratic—or WEIRD—backgrounds, with more than two-thirds of the research coming from America alone (Arnett 2008). If you're an American college student, psychology has had its eye on you pretty much nonstop since the 1950s. But there's comparably little research on the other 88 percent of the world that isn't WEIRD. Humans may be similar worldwide in many ways, but cultures that don't fit neatly into the WEIRD acronym vary significantly in important characteristics ranging from visual perception and spatial reasoning to cooperation and fairness, even the heritability of IQ (Henrich, Heine, and Norenzayan 2010).

Consider the phenomenon of *illusory superiority*—also colorfully known as the *Lake Wobegon effect*, after the fictional town in the radio show *Prairie Home Companion*, where, in spite of statistical impossibility, "all the children are above average." Similarly, the majority of Westerners believe they are better than their average peers when it comes to a wide array of desirable traits including IQ, popularity, job skill, and driving ability, among many others. Right now you may be thinking, "I don't do that, but I know other people who do." The research is one step ahead of you: most people believe they are less susceptible than average to this bias even when it is explicitly explained to them (Pronin and Kugler 2007). Illusory superiority runs so deep that we are literally biased about our own bias. In fact, people who are worst at certain skills often believe they are among the most exceptional (Kruger and Dunning 1999), a phenomenon that has graced us with countless earsplitting episodes of *American Idol*. Yet for all its prevalence in the West, this tendency toward self-enhancement seems conspicuously absent in many East Asian cultures (Heine and Hamamura 2007).

If you're not particularly WEIRD, some of the findings presented here might not resonate with you. Even if you are, keep in mind that science works with large numbers to iron out the wrinkles of subjectivity and draw insights about human happiness as a whole and on average. But there's no such thing as an average individual, and for your particular happiness, all your little quirks and idiosyncrasies make a big difference. They make you *you*. Everything you encounter in this book should be tested in the laboratory of your own life. Some things will fit, others will fall flat. The ways in which you break the mold will be just as illuminating as the ways in which you make the mold. No matter how sophisticated our science gets, the novelist Jane Austen had it right: "You must be the best judge of your own happiness."

A Biased Judge

Just because you're the best judge of your happiness that we've got doesn't mean you're flawless. The phenomenon of illusory superiority shows us just one way we often deceive ourselves about ourselves. There are dozens upon dozens of other cognitive biases to choose from, each clouding our window to the world and our insight into ourselves in its own way.

One bias that's particularly important for those of us hunting for happiness is the *negativity bias*. Negativity bias arises from the fact that your brain is hardwired to pay more attention to bad things than good things, and those bad things hold much more sway on your psychological balance. This fairly innate bias begins showing up as early as three months old

(Hamlin, Wynn, and Bloom 2010). As we age, it expands into a complex web of behaviors and preferences. In experiments that led to a 2002 Nobel Prize, Daniel Kahneman and Amos Tversky demonstrated that people generally hate economic losses about twice as much as they enjoy gains of the same amount (1979; 1984). Research by John Gottman suggests that lasting, happy marriages rely on a ratio of five positive interactions for every negative one before they start sliding toward divorce (1994). In the grimly titled study "Bad Is Stronger than Good," psychologist Roy Baumeister extends the shadow of negativity bias far beyond dollars and divorces and into basic functions, such as what we pay attention to, how we learn, what we remember, and nearly every corner of our behavior, finally concluding that "The self appears to be more strongly motivated to avoid the bad than to embrace the good" (2001, 355).

As much as this bias sounds like a bummer, it has an undoubtable survival value. If you don't stop to take in the sunset the next time you're driving home on a beautiful evening, well, tomorrow's another day. But if you don't stop in time when someone swerves toward you from oncoming traffic, there might be no more sunsets for you at all. As an evolutionary adaptation, negativity bias may keep us primed to avoid perceived threats, but it also leaves us with a tendency to err on the side of perceiving a threat whether or not one actually exists. From behind the lens of negativity, a lot of the good stuff slips by us without actually sinking in. Neuropsychologist Rick Hanson uses the analogy that negativity bias makes the brain like Velcro for the bad and Teflon for the good (2013). In the chapters ahead, we'll look at many ways to make happiness stickier and to help untangle ourselves from negativity.

Happiness Yesterday

No matter how skewed your lunch date's perception may be, we actually have no way to prove that our love-struck companion isn't really "*soooooo* happy." But before we let our smitten friend off the hook entirely, let's look a little closer. While our imperfect estimation of our happiness here and now in the present moment is the best we've got, once the mind wanders toward the past or the future, all sorts of things start to go awry.

In an experiment only a psychologist could devise, Daniel Kahneman studied patients undergoing colonoscopies. A colonoscopy, as anyone who has had one can tell you, is a highly unpleasant procedure involving several feet of tubing and your lower digestive tract. It can last anywhere from five minutes to an hour, and if I were to ask you to pick whether you wanted the short colonoscopy or the long one, which would you choose? Me too. So when Kahneman evaluated patients after the procedure, his first surprise was to find that their reported discomfort looking back had almost no connection to how long the procedure was. But it had a very high correlation with how painful the procedure had been at the end. In fact, his experiment showed that when physicians *added* an extra minute or two to the end of the procedure without moving the scope, patients routinely preferred it to a shorter procedure with a more abrupt end (Redelmeier, Katz, and Kahneman 2003). To the brain, how an activity ends makes a great difference in how the entire event is remembered. So next time you have to get that colonoscopy, ask your doctor to take it easy on the home stretch. Kahneman's experiment and many others like it demonstrate a cognitive bias called the *peak/end effect*, which reveals our memory to be highly sensitive to the final moments of an event, even to the point of overshadowing what has come before. From fireworks to circus acts, there's good reason to go out with a bang.

When I go out to dinner with my wife, I have a ritual of sorts that she affectionately calls "last taste." Wherever we eat, we always share each other's plates, making bites for each other and grabbing morsels from one another throughout dinner. But at some point during the meal, I will craft a special bite full of all the tastiest bits, and set it aside on my plate until the very end. This bite is off limits, and stealing someone's "last taste" is, in our household, the most treasonous of dinnertime crimes. Be warned: if you start to seriously study happiness, these kinds of neurotic antics become part of your daily routine.

Happiness Tomorrow

Sadly, when it comes to our emotions, we don't do a much better job while looking in the other direction either. Psychologists Timothy Wilson and Daniel Gilbert study *affective forecasting*, which is how well we anticipate how we'll feel after something happens in the future. Their studies chronicled almost every delight and downer you can imagine, from "romantic breakups, personal insults, sports victories, electoral defeats, parachute jumps, failures to lose weight, reading tragic stories, and learning the results of pregnancy and HIV tests" (2003, 353). With few exceptions, they found that we tend to imagine both our joys and sorrows as more intense and more enduring than we actually experience them to be.

This phenomenon, known as *impact bias*, held true even for events people had experienced many times before. No matter how many times our team has won or lost, we tend to exaggerate the agony of the impending defeat or thrill of the awaiting victory. Wilson and Gilbert attribute this to what they call our "psychological immune system," a hardwired tendency for the mind to recover from events both good and bad, and then return to equilibrium. They found we tend to underestimate our psychological immune system the most when it comes to negative events. We anticipate the hurt very well, but we anticipate the healing very poorly.

These are just a few cognitive biases that skew our perceptions of the past, present, and future. They and dozens of others color every corner of consciousness, yet in spite of it all we walk through the world under the illusion that the reality we're experiencing is unfiltered, and the self we experience is exactly as it seems. Nothing could be farther from the truth. In terms of our emotions, we can tell when we're feeling sunny, but when it comes to forecasting, we're lousy meteorologists.

~

INQUIRY: THE EMOTIONAL ALMANAC

Think back on one or two moments in your life when you were anticipating a negative event that turned out not to be as bad as you imagined. What was missing from your emotional forecast? What coping strategies, support systems, or aspects of your psychological immune system made a difference that you hadn't anticipated?

Now call to mind an event in the future that you are currently worried about. Imagine how you would feel if it came to pass. Now imagine how you might use some of the same strategies and support systems.

What Is Happiness?

Like philosophers, positive psychologists have a variety of different ways of accounting for all the components of happiness. Momentary positive emotions such as joy, curiosity, and contentment certainly factor into happiness (which is a relief, since anyone who would define happiness without including joy is going to be a real wet blanket). Broader life concepts like flourishing, virtue, and sense of purpose also play an important role in happiness. We might add many more, but for ease of exploration, positive psychology pioneer Martin Seligman distills these topics down to three functional categories: *pleasure*, *meaning*, and *engagement* (2002).

Pleasure

Pleasures are a slam dunk. All the goodies pile up in this category: the first bite of ice cream, settling into a hot bath, dancing to your favorite music. Pleasures are in the moment and often physical. No one needs to read a book to understand what pleasure is (that is the opposite of pleasure). Just the word itself will often send the mind wandering off to imagine a few of our favorite things (or make us put a book down and sneak to the kitchen to grab a bite of something sweet). Which highlights an important flip side to pleasures: they have a strange hold on the mind, and we often go to great lengths to experience them and retain them, even to the point of causing unhappiness.

This is due partly to the inherently fleeting nature of pleasure and the fact that, rather than accumulating, pleasure diminishes as we partake of it. In economics this is called *diminishing marginal utility*, because economists can invent a complicated name for anything. Psychologists gave the same process the classier title *hedonic adaptation*, after Hedone, the Greek goddess of pleasure, known throughout Olympus as a notoriously fickle friend. Marcel Proust immortalized hedonic adaptation better than any other in a scene from *Remembrance of Things Past* that describes the rapture of eating a small cake called a petit madeleine soaked in a cup of tea:

> *No sooner had the warm liquid, and the crumbs with it, touched my palate, a shudder ran through my whole body, and I stopped, intent upon the extraordinary changes that were taking place. An exquisite pleasure had invaded my senses... And at once the vicissitudes of life had become indifferent to me, its disasters innocuous, its brevity illusory—this new sensation having had on me the effect which love has of filling me with a precious essence... I drink a second mouthful, in which I find nothing more than in the first, a third, which gives me rather less than the second. It is time to stop; the potion is losing its magic.* (1922, 58)

Proust highlights the way that pleasures tug on a complex web of history and biology unique to each of us, making them intensely personal and powerful. If you ask me, a mouthful of soggy cake just sounds gross, but substitute a milkshake for a madeleine and I totally get where he's coming from.

Hedonic adaptation plays out in the brain not just for momentary pleasures but for major life events as well. An influential study on lottery winners found that after an initial spike in happiness, winners were not significantly happier one year later than a control group of nonwinners from the same area (Brickman, Coates, and Janoff-Bulman 1978). Remember the psychological immune system? It's hard at work in times like these too, bringing us back to equilibrium from both highs and lows. Regardless of where you get your kicks, whatever wows you will eventually wane. And while the effect is not always immediate, sooner or later it is inevitable. We'll come back to the paradoxes of pleasure throughout this book but, for now, just watch it with the fancy cakes and scratch-off tickets.

In Search of Something More?

With pleasure alone, happiness looks like a pretty shallow pool. If you're desiring deeper waters, say hello to philosopher Robert Nozick. In a famous thought experiment from his book *Anarchy, State, and Utopia*, Nozick asks us to imagine the possibility of being hooked up to a machine that creates any experience we like, anytime. You could experience infinite pleasures at will, and the best part is, you'd never even know you were hooked up, so it would feel just like the real thing. If you're thinking, "Sign me up!" consider this: about as close as science has come to Nozick's machine was an experiment by James Olds and Peter Milner in which rats were allowed to directly stimulate a pleasure center in the brain called the septal area by pressing a lever connected to an electrode. The rats would eventually press the lever up to 700 times an hour, foregoing food and water until they collapsed from exhaustion (1954). Careful what you wish for.

If pleasure were the only source of happiness, there'd be a line around the block for Nozick's machine, yet most people imagine they would turn down such an offer. Nozick concludes that one of the chief reasons we might hesitate over his imaginary contraption is that "there is no *actual* contact with any deeper reality, though the experience of it can be simulated. Many persons desire to leave themselves open to such contact and to a plumbing of deeper significance" (1974, 43). Pleasures inevitably fade and leave us scrambling on an emotional treadmill just to keep up. We want to be engaged with a world outside ourselves, not just sucking down tea and cakes all day long. The "deeper significance" beyond pleasure that Nozick describes requires a happiness that connects us to one another and endures beyond the fading moment. Finding such a happiness calls up the concepts of meaning and engagement.

Meaning

Meaning is the umbrella under which psychologists explore what it is to have a sense of purpose in life greater than one's inner experience and how we strive to achieve or align with it. Whereas pleasures simply feel good, meaning gives us the sense that we have made a difference in the lives of others and the world at large. This concept is articulated beautifully in *Man's Search for Meaning* by psychiatrist and Holocaust survivor Viktor Frankl, who believes it is not satisfied pleasure at all but meaningful purpose that is the root of our happiness:

> *What man actually needs is not a tensionless state but rather the striving and struggling for some goal worthy of him. What he needs is not the discharge of tension at any cost, but the call of a potential meaning waiting to be fulfilled by him.* (1985, 166)

Like Aristotle's *eudaemonia*, Frankl's construct of meaning implies an active state, a reaching out into the world that also requires us to cultivate an introspective ability to, as Frankl writes, "listen to what your conscience commands you to do and go on to carry it out to the best of your knowledge" (1985, 16). Discovering a sense of purpose and striving to carry it out plays a vital role in emotional well-being (Zika and Chamberlain 1992; Reker, Peacock, and Wong 1987). Like pleasures, meanings are as diverse and varied as individuals, and they form in the same enigmatic alchemy of our biology, background, and behavior.

Finding a meaningful path through this lifetime is a central project of yoga practice. It's also the cornerstone of the second half of this book, beginning with the chapter on *dharma* and weaving through the following chapters on how we relate to others, our past, and our future.

Engagement

Engagement is where pleasure and meaning overlap. Each of us has activities we love, favorite hobbies or sports, long conversations with a best friend during which we find ourselves immersed and deeply absorbed. Things that engage us are similar to pleasures in that they feel good to us intrinsically, but like meaning they also challenge us to grow by drawing on strengths and skills essential to who we are.

For example, much as I love a good milkshake, there's not much skill involved there. As long as I can work a straw and keep the stuff off my shirt, it's pretty much a no-brainer. That's clearly a pleasure. But I also love learning in a way that's palpably different than milkshakes. Growing up, I felt awe and admiration for teachers who could take a complex idea and shape it in a way that made it "click" for me, and I felt wonder at how a powerful new idea could reshape my whole understanding of the world. Now, as a teacher of yoga, I spend hours reshaping and rearranging lessons, looking for just the right language or imaginative example to bring that "click" to other people. When that happens, I can feel the delight in my body as my pulse quickens and something electric seems to move in my spine. When I miss the mark, I instantly want to circle back and try another approach. The challenge of teaching is central to why I find it so engaging. Teaching tests and hones skills I value in myself, and hopefully it makes a difference in people around me.

Some of the most extensive and pioneering studies on engagement came from the work of Mihaly Csikszentmihalyi. He is careful to distinguish between a simple pleasure and something more engaging, which he calls enjoyment:

> *After an enjoyable event, we know that we have changed, that our self has grown: in some respect, we have become more complex as a result of it... Experiences that give pleasure can also give enjoyment, but the two sensations are quite different... we can experience pleasure without any investment of psychic energy, whereas enjoyment happens only as a result of unusual investments of attention. A person can feel pleasure without any effort... But it is impossible to enjoy a tennis game, a book, or a conversation unless attention is fully concentrated.* (1990, 46)

Engagement requires an investment of attention and effort beyond pleasure, and the return on that investment is a sense of accomplishment that also reshapes our sense of who we are. Csikszentmihalyi termed this overall process of deep absorption in self-transcending experiences *flow*. He found its pivotal presence in almost all of the activities that people say make them happiest. The absorption of attention is also an integral skill in yoga practice; in fact, one traditional definition of yoga is simply that: the sustained, deep absorption of attention. Through the practices in this book, we will unfold a powerful, pragmatic road map for harnessing attention and learning to cultivate the kinds of flow experiences that are central to a happy life. We'll begin to draw that map with the tools of meditation in the third chapter, then apply those tools to transforming the self and enjoying the present moment in the fourth and fifth chapters.

INQUIRY: A FEW OF YOUR FAVORITE THINGS

Take out paper and a pen and set a timer for five minutes. Write down as many sources of happiness in your life as you can think of. Anything at all, from people to places to things to activities or ideas. As before, try not to censor or second-guess yourself; simply allow thoughts to emerge and record them as they come.

Now, take out another piece of paper and put three columns at the top, one each for pleasure, meaning, and engagement. Begin to place the things that make you feel happy in the column you feel fits best. Pleasure, meaning, and engagement are not mutually exclusive, so certain things may go in more than one column. In fact, you may find that a few of your most treasured sources of happiness fill up all three columns. Are there areas where you feel life is abundant? Places you feel it's lacking? As best you can, compile the list without judgment, simply acknowledging thoughts as they occur.

Together, pleasure, meaning, and engagement offer a broad palette of emotions and experiences, and between the three we could paint infinite portraits of what happiness looks like. The practices presented in this book offer brushes for each color on that palette that you can use to create your own expression of happiness. In the coming chapters, we'll study how to handle them. Some may become trusty tools for everyday use, some may be taken up in a special moment, and others you will set aside for now. After all, happiness is not a paint-by-numbers endeavor. As Proust himself said when his mouth wasn't full of cake, "We don't receive wisdom; we must discover it for ourselves after a journey that no one can take for us or spare us." Deciding what to paint is the great challenge and privilege of a lifetime, and the canvas is calling.

CHAPTER 2

Yoga:
The Battlefield of the Self

Action may not always bring happiness, but there is no happiness without action.

—William James, psychologist and philosopher

Mystics, philosophers, psychologists, and scientists approach happiness and the human experience from different points of entry, but once they're through the door they all discover a house divided. The Buddha, in his *Taming the Mind*, used the image of the mind as a wild forest elephant that must be tied to a stake and trained by our higher faculties. Plato, in *Phaedrus*, used the image of a chariot ascribing the role of the driver to the soul, forever struggling to rein in two horses: one noble, embodying reason, and another wicked, representing the passions. Jump to modern psychology and you'll find Freud's construct of the ego caught between the unconscious, instinctual id and the moral superego (Haidt 2006).

Peek into neuroscience and you'll find similar divisions built right into the architecture of our brains. Neuroscientist Paul MacLean popularized a three-part model for the evolution of the human brain by tracking structures that developed over hundreds of millions of years. The oldest is the *reptilian brain*, which includes structures responsible for instinctive and automatic survival behaviors. Surrounding that is the *limbic system*, common to most mammals, which contains the primary structures for emotions and long-term memories. These structures, especially the hypothalamus, are responsible for what psychologists affectionately call the four Fs: fight, flight, feeding, and...reproduction. The most recent and most quintessentially human part of the brain is the *neocortex*, where we find key structures for activities like conscious thought, future planning, and reasoning.

The sobering truth is this: in the neighborhood of the brain, conscious attention and all the other things that folks like Buddha, Plato, and Freud rely upon to train our egos and elephants are the new kids on the block. The elephant, the id, and the passions have been dwelling in this house for millions and millions of years, all churning away deep inside, while conscious attention struggles to steer one little thought at a time.

With the deck stacked against us like this, it can be tempting to chuck the whole project and let the chips fall where they may. After all, if you can't trust your brain, who can you trust? If you're feeling just a touch down about this whole pursuit of happiness, then yoga has the perfect story for you. It is the Bhagavad Gita, and it starts with our hero, the young warrior Arjuna, sitting disillusioned in the dirt with no idea where to go or what to do.

The Bhagavad Gita

At least 2,200 years old, the Bhagavad Gita is a poem at the center of a larger epic called the Mahabharata, one of the world's largest stories, in which kings and queens intermingle and intermarry with gods and goddesses, with an abundance of intrigue, betrayal, and sacrifice along the way. The story centers on a royal family split into two quarreling factions, with Arjuna at the center of the five Pandava brothers pitted against the one hundred sons of the Kauravas. Each side claims the kingdom for its own. The hostilities between the families grow to a head when the eldest Pandava brother loses the entire kingdom, and eventually his wife and entire family, to a game that the Kauravas have fixed with loaded dice. The Pandavas are banished, sent to wander in the forests for twelve years, only to find further betrayal when they return from exile and are denied reentry to the kingdom. One treachery piles upon another, and war becomes inevitable.

The Bhagavad Gita begins here, on the morning of the greatest battle ever waged. Each side enlisted allies and armies from the farthest reaches and throughout the neighboring lands; scarcely anyone remains neutral. The forces have swelled to nearly four million warriors, gathering in gilded chariots at opposite sides of a great field. The thunder of drums and horns is deafening. Horses are straining at the bit, smelling rage and fear. Blood is about to be shed. Just before the charge is sounded, Arjuna turns to his charioteer and says, "Drive me between these armies and stop. I want to see the warriors I am about to fight, gathered and hungry for battle." (1.21–23)

From the center of the field Arjuna looks to the Pandavas and sees his flesh and blood, his family and kinsmen. Then he looks to the other side of the field, to his enemies the Kauravas, and he sees...his flesh and blood, his family and kinsmen. Arjuna sees *himself* on both sides of the field. He knows whatever blood is shed that day, he will lose his family. He has seen the inevitability of suffering. Shaken by despair and wracked by doubt, Arjuna drops his bow and buckles to the earth. He cannot bring himself to fight:

> "Nothing good can come from destroying my own kinsmen in war. I have no desire for victory or this kingdom or happiness. What good are these things when all those for whom we desire them are ready for battle to give up their fortunes and lives." (1.31–33)

Arjuna's despair is not that he might die. In fact he welcomes death and contemplates allowing himself to be killed by the oncoming armies. Arjuna's anguish is rather that the honor and integrity of his people will be forever stained and broken, no matter what he does. His kinsmen have become so entangled by enmity that Arjuna sees no possibility for the kingdom to be whole again.

Krishna's Counsel

Luckily for Arjuna, the driver of his chariot happens to be Krishna, an incarnation of the god Vishnu. In the pantheon of Hinduism and yoga mythology, it would be tough to find a figure higher up the ladder than

Vishnu, the all-powerful, all-present sustainer and creator of time, existence, and the universe. Krishna is a pretty great guy to hitch a ride with, and it's worth a moment to understand how Arjuna ends up with such an exceptional chauffeur.

As the war brewed, the Kauravas and the Pandavas scoured the kingdom to find warriors and armies willing to fight on their behalf. Krishna was friendly with both families, and his army was excellent beyond compare, so his allegiance was in high demand. Arjuna and one of the Kaurava brothers, Duryodhana, raced to Krishna's home, both determined to win his support. Duryodhana arrived earliest only to discover Krishna still asleep. Reluctant to wake him, but not wanting to lose his chance to appeal to Krishna, Duryodhana took a seat at the head of the bed to wait. Arjuna rushed in next, saw that Duryodhana beat him to it, and obediently sat at the foot of the bed. Then they waited through what we can imagine was a very tense staring contest.

Krishna finally awoke, saw Arjuna sitting at his feet and smiled, "Arjuna! Why have you come to visit me today?" Duryodhana leapt up to interject that he came first so the request is rightfully his to make. Krishna cleverly stopped him: "Well, I saw Arjuna first, so I will hear his request first. But I have known both your families, and I do not want to fight in this battle. So one of you may have my army and its might, while the other can have my counsel in the battle, but I will not fight for you... Now, Arjuna, what would you have?"

The choice at hand is pivotal: Which would you rather have? A god's guidance and wisdom, or his might on earth? Both men knew that Krishna is reputed to be the incarnation of Vishnu, but Duryodhana had his doubts. Without hesitation, Arjuna passed up the enviable power of Krishna's army and chose his guidance. Duryodhana, certain of victory now more than ever, raced home gleefully to tell his brothers what a moron Arjuna was.

The Call to Arms

Back on the field of battle, Arjuna is having his darkest moment on his biggest day. Bowed in despair, he turns at last to Krishna and asks for the guidance that he sacrificed so much to receive. Krishna sees his friend's suffering, and this is his reply:

Do not waver in the face of your duty.

For a warrior, there is no higher calling than to fight for what is right.

Warriors given a chance like this are blessed with an open gate to heaven,

and should be happy to encounter such a battle. (2.31–32)

Krishna's battle cry is both rousing and problematic. However much we may know of yoga practice, the images that come to mind are usually of serene contemplation, not bloody conflict. In many traditions of yoga, nonviolence is a central ethical tenet that leaves little room for bloodshed. Yet Gandhi, India's paragon of nonviolence, held the Bhagavad Gita in such high regard that he was reputed to carry a copy with him at all times. He felt it so valuable that when he was imprisoned he used the time to create a translation of the Gita accessible to everyday people throughout India. Why, then, do we find the avatar of a god and the embodiment of yoga giving our hero a kick in the pants toward the battlefield? Gandhi's own explanation of this paradox opens an illuminating window:

…when I first became acquainted with the Gita, I felt that it was not a historical work, but that, under the guise of physical warfare, it described the duel that perpetually went on in the hearts of mankind, and that physical warfare was brought in merely to make the description of the internal duel more alluring. (2012, xvii)

In this light, Gandhi invites us to read the Gita as allegory and to see ourselves in its story. We become Arjuna as we turn inward—brave enough to venture onto the battlefield of our own hearts and take an honest look around, but paralyzed by the forces we find there and uncertain what to do. The Gita is a story for any of us who have dared to examine our own souls and found not only the kindness, love, and happiness we are proud to count among our family of emotions but also the jealousy, hatred, and sadness that are equally our kin.

Arjuna's war has come to a head because he and his brothers have dared challenge the status quo. Like Arjuna, when we embark on a quest to change ourselves, when we move in pursuit of happiness, everything within us aligns to engage or oppose the transformation. Arjuna sees in the army gathered against him not only the sworn lifelong enemies he expected but also lifelong friends, dear uncles, even his beloved childhood teacher. Who among us has not experienced the shock of realization when a job or a love that sustained us for so long now begins to torture us, or when a belief that once liberated the heart now imprisons it? If Krishna speaks to us through Arjuna, then the call to arms he offers the young warrior is a call to action for all of us.

Indeed, no one exists without action, even for a moment. We are all driven into action by our own nature. (3.5)

This single word—*action*—is the beating heart of the Gita. When Arjuna says, "Maybe I shouldn't take action," Krishna says, "That's an action." When we catch a sobering glimpse into ourselves and see a whole army of emotions, it's tempting to say, "Maybe I shouldn't try to change things." Krishna would say to us, "Not trying to change things will change things." Everything is always changing—the self is no exception—and we cannot help but play our part. The message of the Gita is that you can't sit this one out, and you'd be a fool to try. And for those of us who dare to contemplate the pursuit of happiness and the possibility of self-transformation, the Gita insists that the question to ask is not whether to act but *how* to act, and specifically: What kinds of actions dissolve suffering rather than compound it? And the Gita's answer to that question is the practice of yoga.

The Roots of Yoga

The word "yoga" derives from the Sanskrit root *yuj*, which means "to unite" or "to yoke," calling up images of farm animals yoked together for labor. If you've never had the frustrating opportunity to yoke a horse and try to plow a field, I cannot say I recommend it. Especially if you're a severely asthmatic fourteen-year-old on a junior high field trip and you're allergic to horses. Thinking of yoga as "yoking" lets us know that there is work to be done; it calls us to action. In fact, Krishna uses the same word to spur Arjuna into battle in the Gita:

> Be alike in pleasure and pain, gain and loss, victory and defeat,
> yoke yourself to battle and you will do no wrong. (2.38)

Krishna uses the Sanskrit word *yujyasva*—literally "yoke yourself"—to motivate Arjuna. At first glance the phrase "yoke yourself to battle" sounds like Krishna is simply telling Arjuna to commit himself to fighting. But beyond the obvious rallying cry, Krishna delivers a deeper clue to the path of yoga: yoking yourself is *how* you battle. The practice of yoga draws together all the aspects of oneself for the work of self-realization and self-transformation.

Stuck on Our Selves

The philosophy laid out in the Gita suggests that all our suffering rests on a single fundamental problem: *we don't understand who we really are.* Centuries before yogis ever began touching their toes, they built an impressive exercise program rooted in understanding consciousness and the nature of existence. In the first chapter, we poked a bunch of holes in the common belief that we see ourselves clearly. Yoga philosophy ups the ante by suggesting that the problem isn't that our cognitive lenses need a good scrub, it's that the "self" we're looking at and looking with is largely an illusion.

It can be easiest to approach this illusion through a metaphor: Imagine a vast ocean, full of waves ebbing and flowing. From these endless churning waters, a drop emerges into the open space of existence. That drop is you. You look at the vastness and you go, "Wow!" Then immediately after that you say, "Wait, who said 'Wow!'?" The yogis called this part of you *buddhi*, the part that observes existence and aspires to understand it. *Buddhi* is that aspect of your consciousness that witnesses and inquires.

This question—"Who said that?"—sparks something new in you that says, "I said that! I'm a drop!" An instant before, you were dissolved in the sea. You *were* the sea. You're still made up of nothing but sea, but now separation makes you something special. Being separate from the sea makes you a *drop*. Yogis call this *ahamkara*, which means "I-maker" in Sanskrit. The *ahamkara* is the part of you that responds to existence by asserting that you, little drop, are something separate from the ocean.

But the *ahamkara* also saddles you with a problem: gravity. If you end up back in the ocean, you won't be a drop anymore. The ocean that was a big *wow!* a moment ago just became a huge threat. Now you push back against anything that brings you closer to dissolving into the ocean and hang on to the stuff that keeps you feeling like a separate, stable drop. This part of you is called *manas*, which is often translated as "mind." *Manas* constantly says, "I like this… I hate that… I really have to do this tomorrow… Remember how great that was?" All day long, the mind spins tale of desires and dislikes, memories and fantasies, telling the stories that make the drop feel safe and separate from everything else.

Every instant of raw experience sparks so many stories that we no longer experience our own existence as it really is. We not only believe the stories, we come to believe that we *are* the stories. We buy into the separateness of the self; we say to ourselves, "I am this body," or "This voice in my head is me." Keeping up the illusion that you are in control of this separate and stable self takes a lot of mental effort when the universe constantly disagrees with you by changing all the time—and changing you in the process.

～～

Inquiry: Take Your Self for a Spin

Find a quiet place to sit comfortably for five minutes. This exercise is simply about noticing aspects of your self in action. There is nothing to fix and nothing to achieve. As the inquiry unfolds, if you can't notice something, let that be what you notice.

Now, close your eyes and bring attention to your senses. Observe the sounds of the space around you. Notice what colors and textures are present to the eyes, even when they are closed. Feel the touch of air and clothing on your skin.

Now, become aware of your body. Can you notice your breath? Where? How far can you trace that feeling into the body? Feel the pull of gravity and the contact of the body against itself and the support beneath you. Feel the beat of your heart. How far can you trace that feeling into the body?

Now, bring attention to your mind. Notice the pattern of your thoughts, passing from one object to another. Observe the thoughts that grow out of what the senses bring in. Notice especially reactions and attractions to those sensations. Notice how you can steer the mind toward one point, then another. Notice how some sensations pull your attention without any effort on your part. Steer the mind toward a past memory. Stay with it and watch it play out. Now steer the mind toward a future plan, and follow where it leads. When the mind moves toward past and future, where do sensations go? When sensations return, where do thoughts of past and future go?

Now, draw your focus further inward. As thought, feeling, breath, and sensation come and go, what else is in you? Among all these changing things, is there a part of you that is not changing? Notice whatever there is to notice, and let the noticing be enough.

Finally, take a deep breath in, and release the observation as you exhale with a sigh. Notice how you feel now. Slowly open your eyes and return to the day.

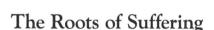

The Roots of Suffering

When we build our sense of self on ground that's perpetually shifting, the inevitable result is suffering. In Sanskrit, the word for "suffering" is *dukha*, which comes from two separate words: *du*, meaning "bad," and *kha*, meaning "space." Originally, the word *kha* described the axle hole of a wagon wheel, and *dukha* referred to a wagon wheel with really shoddy alignment (Sargeant 2009). Similarly, when we're fighting the tide in a sea of constant change, we're in for a bumpy ride.

Yoga philosophy singles out five causes of suffering, called the *kleshas*, or poisons. The cycle starts with our tendency to identify with the thoughts and feelings and stories that surround our experiences. The yogis call this ego, or *asmita*, which refers to the entire architecture of "I and me and mine" that we build with every moment. We do this all the time, as if we met ourselves online and are constantly updating our profiles: "I am tall, I like going out with friends, I also like staying in, I go here, I do this, I like that, I, I, me, me, mine." This kind of self-identification is inevitable and, to a certain extent, essential just for getting through the day. An adequate sense of self is a hallmark of mental health, and when it's missing it can be a major source of mental distress. But the yogis believe that most of us decorate our selves far more ornately than is needed.

All that ego comes with a catch. When an experience happens that shakes the architecture I've erected to hold up my identity, I have to fight back. When I see something that reinforces my sense of self, I have to hang on to it. This is aversion (*dvesa*) and attachment (*raga*). The push and pull of attachment and aversion plays out in our daily lives in abundant, intricate ways. Ever found yourself fishing for a compliment? There's *raga*. Ever seen someone who couldn't take a compliment? There's *dvesa*. An experience occurs, and we add on another story. We even make stories about our stories.

All these stories are like bricks in a fortress designed to defend against the same basic fear: that "I" will cease to exist. The yogis called this *abhinivesa*, and it refers not only to a literal fear of dying but the fear that my self cannot survive without the stories. "Who will I be without this person, without looking like this, without having this stuff, without doing these things?" The same fear can show up the other way around as well. "Who will I become if I take this job? If I marry this person? If I move to this place?"

All the other sources of suffering come together in the final *klesha*, known as *avidya*, or ignorance. *Avidya* literally means "not knowing," and it describes how the entire cycle of suffering rests on misapprehension: *you are not your stories*. The stories we use to build a self are often wildly inaccurate; just consider the cognitive biases and happiness myths we explored in the previous chapter. Winning the lottery won't make you happier (Brickman, Coates, and Janoff-Bulman 1978; Kahneman et al. 2006; Kahneman and Deaton 2010). Neither will moving somewhere warm and sunny (Schkade and Kahneman 1998). The list goes on and on. The suffering (*dukha*) described in yoga philosophy has less to do with physical or mental pain and more with the fact that a self built on stories can never really satisfy because it doesn't stack up with reality. When our stories don't stack up, we find stranger and more specific ones to fill in the cracks. I have a friend who fawns over my cat endlessly and is always the first to volunteer to cat-sit when I'm away. When I asked why she didn't get a cat, this was her genuine reply: "I'm a dog person. I'm worried about who I'd become if I had a cat."

When Krishna holds out relief from suffering, he is not promising a pain-free life of endless pleasure. This is a crucial point in understanding what yoga really offers: the Bhagavad Gita describes a path toward understanding your own existence *as it really is*, and building a life that works harmoniously with the nature of things. Look again at Krishna's command to Arjuna:

Become alike in pleasure and pain, gain and loss, victory and defeat,

yoke yourself to battle and you will do no wrong. (2.38)

Krishna isn't saying yoga will make pain go away. He's not even saying Arjuna will win the battle. He's saying that there is a way to experience pleasure and pain, victory and defeat, without being constantly pushed and pulled by them, and to act from a sense of self less burdened by stories and scarred by circumstance. In the practice of yoga, we're not out to change the nature of the world but rather our reaction to it. Most important, Krishna tells us this process happens on the battlefield, not by sitting on the sidelines.

Inquiry: Shining a Light

Set aside a few minutes to contemplate an area in your life in which you feel suffering, struggle, or like things don't fit right. Use the infinitely regressive why to begin tracing the feeling backward. Can you find traces of the *kleshas* in your own experience? As you observe your thought process, remind yourself that you are not here right now to fix or change what you find. Let the noticing be enough right now. There's no need to figure out what to do or decide whether a situation or thought is good or bad. It's simply about digging up the roots of suffering in your real life. Feel free to let the mind run a little wild here—you may find some surprising, even absurd, stories at work underneath the surface.

~~~~~~

Patanjali's Yoga Sutras

Yoga is a technique for working backward through the stories to that moment of simple experience. It's the process of finding our way back to *wow!* To get a handle on how that process unfolds, we need to introduce another guide who'll be joining us throughout this book: Patanjali. Some yoga traditions believe Patanjali to be the incarnation of the mythical serpent god Ananta. In later medieval accounts he was a Sanskrit grammar teacher. Between snake god and grammar teacher, that's a pretty broad character description. While the truth behind the legend is likely lost forever, the text he left behind, the *Yoga Sutras*, has been revered for more than a millennia for its illuminating instruction on the practice of yoga. In Sanskrit, *sutra* means "thread," and the *Yoga Sutras* are meant to tie together our understanding of what yoga is and how to do it, all in only 196 tidy little lines. With precious little space to get his message across, Patanjali skips the stories and gets right down to the point:

Now, this is the inquiry of Yoga

Yoga stills the movements of consciousness.

Then the Self appears in its essence.

Otherwise, the movements of consciousness appear to be the Self.
(1.1–4)

Right out of the gate, Patanjali's yoga lines up with the problem Krishna put to Arjuna in the Gita: you can't see who you really are. Like water, when the contents of consciousness are in motion, all you can see is surface. The constant waves of thought and the endless flow of feeling seem like all you are. But in these first sutras, Patanjali promises there's much more to you than meets the mind—something he calls an "essence." He deliberately places this essence beneath the movements of the mind and beyond the fluctuations of feeling and thinking and doing and language.

How might we begin to discern who we really are, when Patanjali takes every familiar tool off the table? Even pinning a word on this essence is problematic, as language immediately starts the mind spinning out stories, and whatever Patanjali's pointing toward, he's clearly pointing in the opposite direction of our stories. Many translators use words like "soul," "spirit," "pure awareness," or "emptiness" here, but I've chosen to use the word "Self" with a capital S precisely because it doesn't latch on to any familiar concepts we might be carrying around from other places. But what *is* the Self? Patanjali says there's one way to find out: stillness. We might say that Patanjali's definition of yoga could be condensed into the phrase "stilling toward the Self." To help us get settled, Patanjali lays out a path in eight limbs, or parts.

The Eight Limbs of Yoga

Yama: Ethics relating to others

Niyamas: Virtues relating to oneself

Asana: Posture

Pranayama: Breath regulation

Pratyahara: Sense withdrawal

Dharana: Concentration

Dhyana: Absorption

Samadhi: Illumination

You can see how Patanjali organizes the practice of yoga to escort our awareness progressively farther and farther inward. First, he encourages us to manage our affairs with others and care for ourselves properly; this way, the mind is less likely to be riled up by distractions from the outside. Then, we adjust our posture and breathing to reduce distractions from the inside, freeing attention to withdraw from other things and concentrate. Patanjali promises that through meditation, the mind becomes so absorbed in what we're focusing on that all the usual trappings of the self begin to dissolve, and in a moment of illumination we're able to see the Self as it really is. If this all looks deceptively simple on paper, don't worry. We'll spend the whole rest of the book expanding on the practices of meditation, and you've got the rest of your life to work on it. It should take at least that long.

Together with Krishna and the Gita, Patanjali and the *Sutras* will join us as we delve beneath the surface of ourselves. At first, they seem like an odd couple: Krishna's first command to Arjuna in the Gita is essentially, "Don't just sit there, do something," but Patanjali opens the *Sutras* by telling us "Don't just do something, sit there." Yet together they are like two sides of the same coin. Patanjali wants to lead us inward to the Self, and Krishna wants to show us a way to put that Self out into action in the world.

Into the Breach

Back on the battlefield, peering out from our own chariot, we see ourselves divided, just as Arjuna found his family divided. Once we get a good look at the battle inside our own minds, at all the biases and sources of suffering, if we too feel a bit lost like Arjuna, who can blame us? He's one warrior with a bow in a sea of four million soldiers. Armed only with our conscious attention, we are holding a tiny candle, searching for the Self in the vast dark. In this kind of chaos, what hope is there for happiness? This is why the Bhagavad Gita has to begin with despair. With odds like these, you'd be crazy not to question the fight. Yet the Gita also reminds us that you cannot sit on the sidelines of your own life. In the following chapter we'll learn how the yoga practice of meditation turns that tiny candle of attention into a torch, growing the light of awareness and training the mind to illuminate more and more of who we are, and who we may become.

CHAPTER 3

Meditation: Meet Your Mind

Until you make the unconscious conscious, it will direct your life and you will call it fate.

—Carl Jung, psychologist

It was nearly midnight. I was convinced that someone was going to steal my luggage, and it was totally ruining my attempt to achieve enlightenment before I went to bed. I'd arrived late, courtesy of Manhattan traffic, on my first stay at Kripalu—an erstwhile ashram turned retreat center in the Berkshires of Massachusetts—and I was about to embark on my first meditation retreat. Five days of no talking, early to bed, early to rise, ten-hour daily meditations with nothing to do but come face to face with absolute bliss. Or total emptiness, depending on who you asked. This was serious business for experienced adventurers in the terrain of the brain.

My dirty secret was that I had never *actually* meditated. At that point in my life, I was all about the toe-touching part of yoga. Even when my yoga teacher back home led meditation at the close of class, I usually used the time to check a couple items off my mental to-do list, or tack on a couple extra minutes to the nap at the end. Still, throughout my first months of yoga practice, the benefits of meditation had been dangled out there again and again.

As a tool for training the mind to regulate and monitor attention and emotion, meditation's advertised benefits, depending on the technique, include everything from reduced stress and anxiety (Baer 2003) to increased positive affect (nerd-slang for "happiness") and immune function (Davidson et al. 2003). All this with no apparent side effects—and available for free to anyone with a few minutes a day to spare. More happiness and less flu? Sign me up. It seemed like all carrot and no stick, so I reckoned it was finally time to take a bite. Besides, I fancied myself a quick study. I figured I should be able to pick up meditation pretty easily.

Once I arrived, however, my confidence began to crack just enough to let in a glimmer of apprehension. I decided to spend a little time before bed cramming in the year of meditation experience I'd fibbed about when I applied. I figured half an hour ought to do the trick.

This is how I began to meditate. You are welcome to give it a try for yourself if you like, though I can't say I recommend it.

Inquiry: How Not to Meditate

Sit down.

Try not to think about anything.

If you think about something, stop it.

Continue for half an hour or until you can't take it anymore.

Earlier, when I had checked in at the front desk and asked for my room key, I received a smile instead, along with the reassurance that a key wouldn't be necessary. Apparently one of the last vestiges of Kripalu's ashram days was that none of the rooms had any locks on the doors. For my part, I found the staff's reliance on good vibes quaint but unconvincing. I live in New York; we have thieves so intrepid that my fourth-floor walk-up in Manhattan at the time had bars on the windows and three deadbolts. And I still got robbed. Even so, I decided to play it cool.

This attempt at goodwill lasted all of five seconds into my first meditation, at which point a familiar voice popped into my head and said, *"Someone's going to steal your laptop..."* Shut up. *"Why did you bring it anyway? You can't even use it while you're here."* Really, shut up. *"What do you mean, shut up? I don't do shut up."* Seriously, just be quiet for like half an hour, please. *"You're on my turf now, and if you're gonna sit here for half an hour, you better buckle up because I got a lot to talk about."* Twenty-nine more minutes of this ensued. I was ready to repack my bags and head out, but the next bus wasn't leaving until the following afternoon, so it looked like we were stuck there. Just me and... *me*.

Alone with Your Thoughts?

If we're hoping meditation might make us happier, I really can't stress enough what a bad idea it is to start this way. The first thing my rogue attempt at meditation revealed was that as soon as I tried to clear the deck of thoughts, they came pouring out in droves like rats from a sinking ship. Not only was I having thoughts, I was having thoughts *about my thoughts*. The emptier I tried to get, the more things started to overflow.

I had been convinced since childhood that my body was largely a clunker, but thinking was where I was supposed to be a racecar driver. And now that beautiful brain that had steered me so swiftly through the most complex equations and elegant ideas was careening off course as soon as I asked it to pull over for even a moment. The humbling truth of that would-be meditation was that I really had no idea what was driving my thoughts. But I'd just realized it wasn't me.

Many, many people walk into the practice of meditation for the first time and stumble out with similar stories. Many would prefer not to peek into the mind at all. In fact, researcher Timothy Wilson designed a series of experiments in which he gave participants between six and fifteen minutes simply to be alone with their thoughts in a room free of distraction. Most rated the time as boring and unpleasant. Just how unpleasant? In a later version of the experiment, Wilson gave participants an electric shock beforehand, which subjects said they disliked enough that they would pay to avoid it in the future. Again he left them alone to think, but this time with a button they could press anytime to repeat the same shock that they just said they hated. More than 25 percent of the women and 66 percent of the men pressed the button, many multiple times, including one man who must've had a lot on his mind, because he shocked himself 190 times (Wilson et al. 2014). They didn't *have* to shock themselves, and they didn't *like* the shock, they just decided they liked it more than sitting and thinking. If just being alone with your thoughts for fifteen minutes has you reaching for the button, it might help to understand that you're not actually alone in there. Once we have a better idea what's really going on in the mind, we can build a meditation practice that might actually make a difference.

The Hotel in Your Head

As we saw in the previous chapter, your conscious attention—the "you" that looks around inside—is actually a relatively recent evolution of the brain. It is dwarfed by a mountain of much older automatic and unconscious processes grinding away on their own well beneath the surface of your attention. A good thing too, because if you had to be in charge of everything in your brain, you'd have a very busy day in front of you. Right now, you'd have to remember to take around twelve breaths every minute, and at the same time keep an eye on making your heart beat about seventy times to carry oxygen to your tissues. Then you'd have to focus on aligning more than six hundred muscles in your body in precisely the arrangement required to hold this book steady. Which, by the way, appears upside down when it lands on the retina at the back of your eye, so you'd have to consciously flip it over in your head all the time just to keep the words appearing right side up. You'd also need to meticulously pack up all your memories so you can remember the people you love and find your way back home at the end of the day. I know that's a lot to think about, but if you had breakfast today, please don't forget to digest your food, too, or things will get messy.

It's convenient, to say the least, to have all this daily minutiae taken care of automatically. It's sort of like having a housekeeper and butler who handle all the chores behind the scenes while your conscious attention is out pursuing all the pleasure and meaning of life. If that were all your unconscious mind were up to, I'd encourage you to leave a big fat tip for the staff and get on with the good stuff. But there's a lot more than housekeeping going on behind the scenes.

11,000,000 Rooms: No Vacancy

Just how much of our everyday experience is being handled by the unconscious? In *The User Illusion*, Tor Nørretranders takes a stab at calculating the number of bits (the smallest unit of information) bombarding the brain every second. He then sketches the sheer scale of our unconscious activity:

> The numbers are vast. The eye sends at least ten million bits to the brain every second. The skin sends a million bits a second, the ear one hundred thousand, our smell sensors a further one hundred thousand bits a second, our taste buds perhaps a thousand bits a second. All in all, over eleven million bits a second from the world to our sensory mechanisms. (1998, 125)

And how much of this deluge can be captured in our conscious attention? Nørretranders estimates that it's about 40 bits. Yep, 4–0. As for the other 10,999,960 little tidbits of the universe flooding your brain at every moment, the unconscious mind takes care of all that. If your conscious mind is protesting that it can handle a lot more than 40 measly bits, Nørretranders is one step ahead of you:

> Precisely because from one instant to the next consciousness can switch from one object to another, it is not perceived as limited in its capacity. One moment you are aware of the lack of space in your shoes, the next moment of the expanding universe. Consciousness possesses peerless agility. But that does not change the fact that at any given moment you are not conscious of much at all. (127)

Estimates like Nørretranders's are crude at best, and it's impossible to precisely quantify the volume of information the brain processes in any given moment. Nonetheless, it's clear by any consideration that the scales are tilted massively in favor of the unconscious. Conscious attention processes a small amount of information serially, as a chain of events, while the unconscious processes a vast amount of information in parallel, simultaneously. This is one of the biggest distinctions between the conscious and unconscious mind: *Conscious attention can be in basically one place at one time, while the unconscious handles many things at once.* To manage the flow, the unconscious mind relies on a huge array of diverse structures, overlapping and working in tandem.

You Want to Drive or Should I?

So what does the unconscious *do* with all that equipment? Timothy Wilson, who was giving people electric shocks when we met him a few pages back, writes that the unconscious "gathers information, interprets and evaluates it, and sets goals, quickly and efficiently" (2002, 35). But wait a minute—isn't that all the same stuff consciousness is supposed to be taking care of? Absolutely. It turns out that the conscious and unconscious mind handle some of the same "executive" tasks, even though consciousness likes to think it's steering the mind solo. The problem, says Wilson, is not so much that the unconscious has a hand on the wheel but that it drives by a completely different set of rules:

> [The] *unconscious is an older system designed to scan the environment quickly and detect patterns, especially ones that might pose a danger to the organism. It learns patterns easily but does not unlearn them very well; it is a fairly rigid, inflexible inferencemaker...* [Consciousness] *develops more slowly and never catches up in some respects... But it provides a check-and-balance to the speed and efficiency of nonconscious learning, allowing people to think about and plan more thoughtfully about the future.* (66)

Between them we see two very different systems, built with different skills and guided by different priorities. And as we're about to see, consciousness tends to get into trouble when it tries to drive like the unconscious mind does.

The Myth of Multitasking

Thanks to the miracles of modern technology, today we can watch television while writing an e-mail on the computer while listening to music while texting our pals while talking to grandma on speakerphone while flipping through a menu to decide what to order for delivery. How have we learned to spread our precious conscious attention and accomplish so much more in so much less time? We haven't. I'm sorry to tell you, but you're a horrible multitasker. So am I. Welcome to the club.

We've already seen that conscious attention is hardwired to hold one activity at one time, no matter how hard we try to teach it to juggle. What you and I experience as multitasking—the feeling of consciousness spread evenly and artfully among many different tasks—is actually an illusion that arises from attention jumping from one thing to another repeatedly, and in quick succession, similar to the way we think a movie "moves," even though it's just a rapid progression of still images. (Though we still call it a movie because asking someone out on a date to see a rapid progression of still images is really unromantic.)

Psychologists call this dance of attention *task-switching*, and when we do it, we're worse at just about everything we do. People given math problems drop their speed by as much as 40 percent when they have to multitask (Rubinstein, Meyer, and Evans 2001). Multitasking increases stress (Mark, Gudith, and Klocke 2008). And the more we do it, the worse we seem to be at it (Ophir, Nass, and Wagner 2009). What consciousness learns to do instead of processing tasks simultaneously is to constantly jump back and forth, grabbing onto one thought after another, creating the illusion of a stream of attention from thousands of little drops of thought and feeling. In the process, attention spills way more than it catches, and it smooths over the gaps enough to make it feel like you didn't miss a thing. Our conscious attention is so limited it usually can't even see its own limits. The greatest trick the mind ever played was to fool itself.

Accelerating Attention

To weather the deluge without getting drenched, conscious attention relies on three primary skills: holding information, updating new information, and seeking stimulation (Hanson 2009). How well attention does any of those things depends on how we use it. To find out what we've been up to, let's take a trip to the movies.

When the golden age of film began in the 1930s, the average length of a single cut or "shot" in a feature film was about ten seconds. Today it is about four seconds, and many action films now blitz by at a blistering two seconds per shot. As a result, our movies have gone from about three hundred to seven hundred shots to anywhere between two thousand and four thousand (Bordwell 2002). That means that today's film fans are processing as much as *ten times* as many visual changes as the movie-loving pioneers of yesteryear.

Even without the modern mania for media saturation, this process of attention jumping back and forth would still be happening all the time. You're encountering an impossible amount of information whether you're watching *Keeping Up with the Kardashians* or watching paint dry. What the Kardashians do to your brain that a can of paint doesn't is to bombard your brain with new information and stimulation, while virtually ignoring any need to hold information.

This is not in and of itself a bad thing—being able to handle new information and stimulation has always been a vital survival skill, made increasingly essential by modern life. But as the pace of life accelerates and sources of stimulation proliferate, we get constant training in those skills just getting through the day. In the process, our ability to hold information and keep our focus steady atrophies—so much so that neuroscientists have discovered that in its default or resting state, the brain tends to automatically generate irrelevant neural activity when it doesn't have a sufficiently engaging task, just to give itself new and stimulating information to chew on (Mason et al. 2007). Researchers have given this phenomenon an appropriately fancy name: *stimulus-independent thought*. You and I recognize it as good old-fashioned mind-wandering, and it turns out it's what most of us spend most of our time doing when we think we're doing nothing. All in all, we're thinking about something other than what's actually happening almost *half* the time, and the kicker is that most of that time makes us unhappy (Killingsworth and Gilbert 2010). Sure, a wandering mind has its upsides—a little daydreaming can be great for creativity and planning, for example, and it seems to play an important role in integrating our past and future "selves" (Baird et al. 2012; Smallwood and

Andrews-Hanna 2013). But the bottom line is that a mind that can't hang on to the here and now is destined for unhappiness.

Meanwhile, Back at the Ashram

Which is exactly where I found myself in the middle of the night at Kripalu, with a brain that didn't know how to slow down or stay put or stop looking for the next big thing. That's right where meditation is meant to meet us. While the habits and limits of conscious attention are a big part of what got us into the mess, the power of conscious attention is also what will help us get out. On a fundamental level, engaging in a meditation practice begins a quest to remodel the brain by training and strengthening our innate but underexercised ability to focus attention. While we may spend all our lives in the mansions of our minds, if we're planning to do some renovation in there, we really ought to at least talk to a professional.

Good thing we now have Patanjali on speed dial. Let's look again at the first four lines of the *Yoga Sutras*:

Now, this is the inquiry of Yoga

Yoga stills the movements of consciousness.

Then the Self appears in its essence.

Otherwise, the movements of consciousness appear to be the Self.
(1.1–4)

These first sutras help us navigate around the trap so many beginning meditators fall into when they sit down and try to stop thinking. Patanjali doesn't start by asking us to stop thinking—he's encouraging us to begin by controlling the *movement* of thoughts. Focusing on stopping thought is a surefire way to tangle your brain up in knots. In fact, there is a whole nook of your neural anatomy, the anterior cingulate cortex (ACC), whose job it is to monitor whether you're succeeding in your goals and then to adjust your attention accordingly. But that means that if your goal is not thinking, right out of the gate your ACC automatically lights up and starts thinking about not thinking. Good luck digging your way out of that hole.

Our first challenge in meditation is not to empty the ocean but to calm the current. To do that, we need to give the mind something to hang on to, like a flotation device for our focus. We've seen how the mind loves to dart back and forth from one thing to the next, even how it will invent things to play with when there's nothing around that's interesting. In yoga, the meditative journey begins by giving the mind *just one thing*, and teaching it to stay put. This kind of meditation is sometimes referred to simply as concentration, and our first concentration is on the breath.

INQUIRY: MEDITATION ON THE BREATH

Find a time and place where you can sit undisturbed for fifteen minutes; it can be helpful to set a timer so you don't need to track the time. Bring yourself to a comfortable position in which you can sit with a long spine. If you sit on the floor, consider using a cushion to elevate your hips. If you sit in a chair, try to avoid leaning back or slouching. Let your hands rest on your knees or in your lap. Take a few moments to adjust your body, and then close your eyes.

Begin by noticing whatever there is to notice. Sounds from the world around you. Sensations shifting inside your body. Thoughts and feelings passing through your mind. Right now, don't try to push anything away, and don't try to follow anything in particular. If the body needs to adjust, let that happen. If a thought grabs your attention, just acknowledge it. Notice what you notice, and let that be enough.

Now, gradually shift your attention toward your breath. Take a few moments to find and follow the rhythm of your breath with your focus. As much as you can, allow your breath to breathe itself, in and out, without trying to make anything happen. Notice where you feel your breath moving in your body. Is it in your belly? Your chest? Can you feel it in the front of your body? What about the back? Where else can you feel your breath moving? Notice the texture and tempo of your breath. Does it move smoothly, or are there rough patches? Is it even, or is one part of the breath bigger than another? Are there pauses between the inhale and the exhale, or does one breath go right into the next? Does the breath trigger thoughts or feelings elsewhere in the body or in your mind? Notice whatever there is to notice inside the breath. If it feels like you can't notice something, let that be what you notice.

Now, ask your attention to remain with your breath, but gather up all those thoughts about the breath and let them go. Let your mind rest on the simple experience of breathing, and watch your breath as it comes and goes without having to describe or explain it, as best you can.

From time to time, your mind will wander to another thought, or another sensation will pull your focus away. When this happens, notice the thought or the sensation. Acknowledge it and make it the object of your attention for a moment, and then choose to return your attention to your breath. Do not worry if your mind moves away from the breath often; this is normal. Each time you notice the mind has moved from the breath, bring it back without judgment. If the mind wanders one hundred times, bring it back one hundred times.

When fifteen minutes have passed, take a deep breath in, imagine gathering up this entire meditation, and then let it go with a sigh. Slowly allow your attention to expand beyond your breath to other sensations, sounds, and thoughts. When you are ready, open your eyes and return to the day.

Just Keep Coming Back

In meditation we often start with the breath because it is at once familiar and unfamiliar. Take a breath in as you read this sentence and pause to notice what you feel. Chances are you were able to pick out a lot of details inside that breath—you may have even chosen to take a deeper breath or sigh just because you were watching what the breath was doing. But what about the breath right before that? It must have happened, or you'd have passed out, yet because your conscious attention was elsewhere a few moments ago, there are no feelings or facts to recall. The breath that came before, like most of the roughly fifteen thousand breaths you take every day, was controlled by entirely unconscious actions from your brain stem while your consciousness was busy in the cortex with other things. Bring your attention to your breath again, and you are actually breathing with a different part of your brain (Corfield, Murphy, and Guz 1998).

On the one hand, breath is an easily accessible object of attention. You've done it literally millions of times, so when I asked you to take a single breath and notice it, that's the easy part. When meditation asks you to *keep* noticing, that's the hard part. The very familiarity in the breath also makes it a challenging target for attention, with its great attraction to stimulation and novelty, and sooner or later (usually sooner) we're likely to wander away.

Especially early on, when the mind may scarcely stay put for a moment, remember that in this kind of meditation the coming back *is* the meditation. In his 2006 book *The Wisdom of Yoga*, Stephen Cope, founder of Kripalu Institute for Extraordinary Living, compares the mind to a puppy, always sniffing around and constantly chewing on things. When you're trying to train a puppy to sit and stay, if you just hold the puppy down, as soon as you let go, he'll be off again. When we start working with the mind, getting it to stay put isn't the important part; the important part is getting the mind to come back.

And how we come back to the breath makes a big difference. Often when we bring the mind back to the breath, just like a puppy it returns carrying stuff. We get frustrated by our inability to concentrate; mundane or insignificant thoughts might take on epic proportions as the mind tries to justify thinking about anything else but the boring old breath. If we respond by reacting to each new thought or feeling the mind brings back from its wanderings, in essence it's like telling the puppy that once he runs away, if he just brings back something new or interesting enough, then he can go ahead and play.

Punishment doesn't help either. If we yank the mind back toward concentration only to swat ourselves on the nose, that just creates one more movement in the mind. Punishing the mind just starts thoughts and feelings splashing about even more, and the waves grow bigger. Sooner or later, if we want to come back to the breath, we'll have to let those punishing thoughts go too. We know the unconscious is especially primed to latch on to feelings of failure, threat, and punishment via old brain structures like the anterior cingulate and amygdala. Once these areas are activated, they can create mental waves that are much, much harder for our attention to manage or even detect. When our concentration stumbles, sometimes it's the kick we give ourselves that does the most damage.

Instead, when we notice how thoughts are attracted to and distracted from the object of meditation, and we return them firmly but gently, without judgment, we're helping the mind to release its addiction to what's novel and stimulating. And we're strengthening our ability to simply shine the light of attention in whatever direction we choose. When we notice the mind wander, that's not a failure—that's the practice. When we have to bring it back, that's not an admission of defeat—that's the practice. When we come back without judgment—let's say it all together now—*that's the practice.*

Finding Something to Settle On

Meeting the mind without judgment when it comes back keeps us from adding insult to injury; it gives us space to watch the waves of thought come and go without getting drowned in the process. In a meditation of concentration, we are simply honing an innate but often underutilized aspect of consciousness. What we concentrate on may make less of a difference than the simple fact that we are practicing concentration. In the *Yoga Sutras*, Patanjali offers many different fields in the mind where we might plant our attention and see what grows:

Consciousness settles while radiating kindness, compassion, friendliness and equanimity toward all things—pleasant and painful, good and bad.

Or while lingering in the space between breaths.

Or when steadily observing arising sensations.

Or by focusing on thoughts that are illuminating and free from sorrow.

Or on anything that does not inspire attachment.

Or in the contemplation of sleep and dreaming.

Or through meditation on any chosen object.

Consciousness may become absorbed in anything, immense or insignificant. (1.33–40)

Patanjali offers emotions, breath, sensations, memories, even dreams as suitable soil for meditation, and in case that weren't enough to get us started, he finishes the list by suggesting that we can learn to settle the mind using nearly any object at all. Breath is just one place to begin; Patanjali lets us know that the doorways to concentration are potentially infinite. If attention can touch it, then we can train the mind to hold on to it.

Unexpected Doorways

As it happened, after my first disastrous meditation back at Kripalu, I got a chance to put Patanjali's promise to the test the very next morning over breakfast. Another holdout from Kripalu's ashram days is the silent breakfast, which offers everyone a chance to ease into the day with a quiet, contemplative meal. Occasionally, the cafeteria would have some kind of ambient, new age music lulling in the background to smooth over the clatter of dishes, but since I'd been sleeping to the lullaby of city sirens for several years, to me the silence was deafening. Even so, that morning I dutifully sat down to practice my meditation on a mindful meal.

At which point a kind of low, distant moan echoed through the cafeteria. I had never heard anything like it before. I can only describe it in retrospect as the sound I imagine a goat would make if it were being slowly strangled: a sort of tortured, fading, "BHAAaaaaahhhh." Surprisingly, the rest of the guests maintained their zen-like composure; I seemed to be the only one who noticed. So I brought my mind back to my breakfast with nonjudgment. A minute later it happened again. Then again, and again, irregularly throughout the meal.

In the years since, I've combed through enough psychology journals to know that if you want to make someone absolutely crazy, a great way to do it is to make him or her listen to an annoying sound that can't be controlled, and then to play it at random intervals. This was working like a charm. By the end of breakfast, I was fresh out of equanimity and desperate to complain to the staff, except that I'd just taken a vow of silence for four more days. Kripalu was haunted by a phantom goat that only I could hear, it had ruined my morning meditation, and I couldn't tell anybody.

It came back the next morning, and the next, the same ghostly "BHAAaaaaahhhh" punctuating moments of quiet that had now become electric with expectation in my mind. I became convinced that the sound was deliberate, that Kripalu was playing some traditional, mystical chant, soothing to everyone but rank spiritual amateurs like myself.

With Patanjali's words echoing in the back of my head, I resolved to meditate on this sacred-goat noise until every last ripple in my consciousness settled. If you can't beat 'em, join 'em. "BHAAaaaaahhhh." I stayed late after breakfast, determined to still the waves of my mind. During other meditations throughout the day, the memory of the sound would sneak in through the cracks in my concentration to annoy me afresh. "BHAAaaaaahhhh."

The next day, I looked forward to it, no longer an itch in my ear, now an anticipation. When it was strangely absent at dinner, I missed it. Not good—I had leaped from the claws of aversion to the waiting arms of attachment. "BHAAaaaaahhhh." By the next morning, I grew certain I could sense a secret beneath the noise. It was probably Swami Kripalu himself, intoning some numinous sound of the universe. Still not good— just more stories my mind was conjuring up. "BHAAaaaaahhhh."

On the final morning I was more or less resigned. Later that day, our retreat would formally break silence, and I'd board a bus back home. I'd watched the patterns of my consciousness flow this way and that, but stillness was nowhere to be found. Pretty much all that was left was to pack up and say good-bye to the ghostly goat I'd been chasing all week. I closed my eyes. "BHAAaaaaahhhh." It was there right on cue, emerging from the quiet chorus of cafeteria sounds, then dissolving again. I just listened for a while as it came and went...

When my eyes sprang open, I realized the cafeteria was almost empty. I felt like I'd passed through some kind of tunnel without going anywhere—it seemed impossible but nearly half an hour had passed on the clock. I hadn't fallen asleep, I'd been right there the whole time, just listening to myself listening.

Just when I'd given up trying, I meditated.

Timed perfectly to my moment of pride and discovery, I happened to glance over at one of the cafeteria workers, who'd just finished cleaning a table and grabbed a cup to make some tea. He strolled down the empty buffet line to the industrial hot-water dispenser at the end and pulled the lever to fill his cup. I think I heard it before it actually happened— "BHAAaaaaahhhh."

I had just spent four solid days meditating on the sound of a broken teapot.

Choose Your Own Adventure

I was embarrassed to admit it, but Patanjali was right. One *can* become absorbed in any object, whether immense or insignificant. Even so, I don't recommend smashing your teapot and starting the stove just to see how it goes for you. Inevitably, for each of us there will be some doorways that open easily to meditation and others that seem impenetrable. There are a multitude of techniques for meditation, and while it may be possible to meditate on anything, what initially works for you will depend largely on the habits and patterns that your unique mind has already developed. It makes sense to begin with a meditation that is engaging and accessible, so you don't have to spend a lot of time banging your head against a wall waiting for it to become a door.

Earlier, we sketched out three basic behaviors of conscious attention: holding information, taking in new information, and seeking stimulation. If your mind feels especially primed toward taking in new information, for example, consider emphasizing the aspects of meditation that require you to notice subtle details in your own experience—not just the rhythm in your breath but its exact location in your body and the precise timing of the muscles that move. Conversely, if you often find yourself battling with anxiety, choosing a place free of distractions and an object that's less stimulating may make a big difference for you. As each of us comes to understand the unique alchemy of our own consciousness, we can cultivate personal meditation techniques that meet us where we are.

At the same time, we need to acknowledge that, like any skill, meditation will require some time to stabilize. My wife is an extraordinary violinist and has been training since she was four. Today she plays an exquisite two-hundred-year-old instrument, but her very first "violin" was a cardboard box with a ruler taped to it. Her teacher always started young students with a cardboard box as they were learning how to hold their arms and fingers, because she knew that along the way they would inevitably grow frustrated and smash their instrument. And to hear her tell it, she smashed quite a few. The problem wasn't in the instrument, it was in the natural impatience of a four-year-old. Her teacher wisely didn't expect her to behave as anything other than a child and therefore adapted the instrument to fit her as she was. She compassionately let her student move through the inevitable frustrations of doing something challenging and unfamiliar. Any way we can do the same for ourselves in meditation will only serve the process.

Practice and Detachment

As we embark toward the challenging and unfamiliar reaches of the mind, Patanjali offers a pair of tools from the *Sutras* to carry on our travels:

The movements of consciousness still with practice and detachment.
(1.12)

The twin virtues of practice and detachment may seem like opposites at first, as if we're being told to hold on and let go at the same time. But the ways practice and detachment intertwine, and the subtle tensions between them, form the foundation for meditation. With practice (*abhyasa*), Patanjali acknowledges that, like any training, the meditative process unfolds through dedication, repetition, and time. As Joseph Campbell reminds us, when you practice, "at first you may find that nothing happens there." Commitment to practice keeps us coming back, again and again, to the breath or wherever we are. Detachment (*vairagya*) keeps us from smashing our instrument before the practice can take root. It's Patanjali's reminder that when we get too hooked on the outcome, all our effort toward stillness simply stirs up more movement. At this point, Krishna chimes in from the battlefield of the Gita to echo Patanjali's encouragement:

Doubtless, Arjuna, the mind is restless and difficult to subdue.

But with practice and detachment it will be mastered in the end.
(6.35)

Like Patanjali, Krishna doesn't pull any punches: changing the mind is difficult. When we start to explore the quirks of consciousness and the unconscious depths beyond, it can feel like the odds are against us. There's a reason why, in the Gita, Arjuna and his four righteous brothers are pitted against one hundred evil cousins. For our own place in the battle, conscious attention is like Arjuna's bow, our weapon in the war, and meditation teaches us how to hold it.

As we learn to hold the mind with practice in one hand and detachment in the other, meditation opens a pathway that will transform the mind, polishing it into something reflective whereby we can catch a glimpse of an essence in each of us, a place beyond breath or thought or feeling, a place where there is truly nowhere else to go and nothing else to do. This is the Self that Patanjali promised, untroubled by the ocean of thought. To undertake that evolution of awareness, we need to understand how transformation takes place.

CHAPTER 4

The Pillars of Transformation

Those who cannot change their minds cannot change anything.

—George Bernard Shaw, playwright
and social critic

I once had this fat old cat named Ralph who hated it when anything changed. He was found hidden and shivering under the stairwell of an abandoned building, where apparently he'd been left by a previous owner for more than a year before I ended up with him. His preferred method for voicing his displeasure when things changed was to pee on them. When I brought him home, he crawled under my bed, peed there, and lived in that spot for a month. I would slide food under the bed when I left in the morning, and when I came home I would find the empty bowl pushed barely out from under the bed. I liked to imagine him nudging it out with his little paw, thinking, "The food's not bad. I still hate you."

One night I came home and he was just napping on the couch as if he'd been happily sleeping there forever, and from then on we were pals and everything was great. Until I went away for a weekend. I'd scarcely set my overnight bag down when he jumped right on top and peed so much I suspected he'd been holding it since Friday. First he hated that I was there, now he hated that I went away.

When I bought a new sofa, I actually thought to myself, "I bet Ralph will pee on this." So I waited a week to unwrap the sofa's plastic covering. Ralph waited too, until ten minutes after I unwrapped it, then he let loose. When my wife and I started dating, after it became clear she'd be a regular fixture in his home, Ralph jumped onto that same couch one evening while we were watching a movie, looked her dead in the eye, and peed. On me. He was nothing if not direct. Mary Shelley famously wrote in *Frankenstein*, "Nothing is so painful to the human mind as a great and sudden change." I like to think she also had a cat like Ralph.

Change permeates the *kleshas*—the sources of suffering we encountered in the second chapter. To uphold the story of my self, I cling to and crave the moments that reinforce the narrative, and I fear the changes that threaten it, hoping to somehow build up a self that might outlast and outrun the biggest and most inevitable change we'll all experience: death. We imagine ourselves as the architects of monuments to weather the test of time, all the while building sandcastles at high tide.

Yet at the same time we long for change. We strive to build a better life—for ourselves, for our children, for our communities. We buckle down to break the bad habit. We pursue happiness. As stung and suffering as we have been by the winds of change, we know that without change and its challenges, we will wither. The paradoxes and possibilities of transformation are the topic of this chapter.

Change Upon Change

In the 1960s, two psychiatrists named Thomas Holmes and Richard Rahe combed through the medical files of more than five thousand people to devise a system for rating the stress caused by life changes and the likelihood that those stresses would lead to later illness (1967). The resulting Holmes and Rahe Stress Scale, which asks you to tally events from the past year of your life to evaluate your overall stress level, proved quite reliable and is still used in various forms today. Their surprising discovery was that not only do unexpected and painful changes increase stress and resulting illness, but so do *any* significant changes. Just got fired? Bummer, that'll add 47 points to your stress scale. But you're about to get married, so that should make everything better, right? Actually, getting married clocks in at a 50, which means it's likely to stress you out just a bit *more* than losing your job. Did you have an "outstanding personal achievement?"

Congratulations, that adds 28 points to your stress total—just a little less than fighting with your in-laws, which tacks on 29 more.

The Stress Response

It would be many years before the underlying mechanism was uncovered. When something threatens our sense of psychological equilibrium, a cascade of activity begins from the hypothalamus to the pituitary to adrenal glands, which flood the body with stress hormones like cortisol and epinephrine. These hormones elevate heart rate and blood pressure, putting the body in a state of hyperalert. All of that is great in a crisis, or any time we really need all our physical and attentional resources online and ready to go, but cortisol also has the side effect of inhibiting immune function in the long run, providing the link between stress and illness that Holmes and Rahe observed.

The genius of the stress scale is its acknowledgment that our bodies and minds process changes of all kinds, both good and bad, through the same structures. Graduating from school, falling in love, buying a home, starting a family—for many of us these are life's pinnacle events. Yet each and every one of them radically reshapes the story of our selves. Rewriting our stories, even when they take a happy turn, thrusts us into a place of temporary disorientation. We look for the familiar markers around and inside ourselves and find them altered or missing. We no longer know who we are with such certainty. Our organism goes on high alert as we endeavor to adapt to the change, but our biology can only handle so much before we start to buckle from the pressure.

Destined to Develop

Yet under the right kind and amount of stress, life not only endures but flourishes. Consider exercise: you want to become stronger so you head to the gym, then sweat and grunt from the stress until you can't run another mile or do another push-up. If you take the short view, strength training is the stupidest idea man has ever come up with: you leave weaker than when you walked into the gym. But then something vital within you kicks into gear, and, gradually, over days and months, you emerge stronger, faster, more capable. You have become more alive.

The ability for an organism to adapt and change itself in the presence of stress is a fundamental and unique characteristic of life itself. A rubber band never grows more rubbery with stretching. Chiseling a stone cannot make it stonier. Under stress, inanimate objects cannot grow. But you can. Nobody knows why life has to exist in this pattern, when the rest of the vast inanimate universe ignores it. But we ignore it in ourselves at our own peril, and without the requisite stimulation our muscles weaken, our organs waste, and our vitality wanes.

The desire to change things seems embedded in us from birth, or close to it. From the moment he was able to sit up at just a few months old, my son had a relentless fascination with knocking things over. It didn't matter what it was—a stack of blocks, or books, or, one unhappy time, a pile of clean dishes—if he could reach something stacked on top of something else, he was determined to knock it down. Once when he was learning to walk, he took a particularly hard tumble that resulted in howling and tears impervious to hugs. Out of desperation I started stacking up his alphabet blocks as fast and high as I could until he stopped bawling and began a precise, complex infant calculation: *I can keep crying, or I can knock down that awesome tower.* Sure enough, the tears lost and he toddled over just to marvel at the fact that he could change something in the world.

Psychologist Robert White found this kind of behavior universal in children and adults alike—a need to alter our environment with a sense of competence, which he called *effectance motivation* (1959). Unlike biological needs such as hunger and thirst, effectance motivation serves not to make up for something we lack but to enhance our innate abilities and improve ourselves. Since effectance motivation and the broader need for self-efficacy are driven by growth rather than compensating for a deficit, they can never be fully satisfied. If he could talk, my son would have told you that there are never enough blocks to knock over.

But of course you and I don't feel an insatiable desire to topple every tower we come across (okay, maybe just a little). That's because, while the basic drive stays with us, effectance motivation is expressed through increasingly complex behaviors as our skills and abilities evolve throughout a lifetime. Thus, as adults we end up like early mountaineer George Mallory, climbing Mount Everest simply "because it's there." A later study suggests that Mallory was not just being glib—a major motivator for climbers of all stripes is the sense of competence and control it provides (Ewert 1985). Even my son, though he's not yet scaling Everest, recently retired his passion for knocking things over and has moved on to his next great frontier: stacking things. Our house is much cleaner now.

Our drive to action has important consequences for our health and well-being. Drawing on White's theories, psychologist Albert Bandura later coined the term *self-efficacy* to describe "people's beliefs in their capabilities to produce desired effects by their own actions" (1997, vii). A positive sense of self-efficacy has profound effects on our health: it strengthens immune response and stimulates the release of endorphins, which are natural painkillers, as well as catecholamines, a group of neurotransmitters vital for managing stress (Bandura 1997; O'Leary 1992). On a larger level, Bandura found that as effectance motivation stimulates behaviors, those behaviors become a complex web of beliefs about what we can and can't accomplish in the world, and those beliefs in turn either empower or inhibit future behaviors. Bandura's seminal body of research indicates that self-efficacy plays a key role in our ability to initiate changes in our lives and maintain behavior in the face of challenges. And while effectance motivation may be innate, one's sense of self-efficacy is not a genetic trait but an acquired belief system shaped by a lifetime of experience (Bandura 1977). First we make our choices, then our choices make us.

Karma and Samskara

All of this would come as no surprise to Krishna and Patanjali. The Gita hits the nail right on the head when it comes to our relationship to action.

No one exists without action, even for the slightest instant.

All are drawn to action, even against their will, by their very nature.
(3.5)

According to yoga philosophy, our actions—everything we do in every moment—change us constantly and ceaselessly, through the law of *karma*. Easily the most popular idea to make the leap from ancient yoga philosophy to everyday conversation, *karma* is also probably the concept that's gotten the most mangled up along the way. *Karma* does not refer to some kind of elaborate divine retribution, wherein if you don't tip the barista at the coffee shop, then somewhere halfway around the world Krishna tells a butterfly to flap its wings on the Swiss Alps, which makes a mountain goat sneeze, triggering an avalanche that buries a group of vacationing celebrities, causing your favorite television show to be canceled.

The Sanskrit root of *karma* means "to do or enact," and to understand its meaning we need to pair it with another word, *samskara*, which means "impression." Together, *karma* and *samskara* refer to a psychological cause and effect that continually shape who we are and who we become. According to the yogis, every action we take, even our thoughts and intentions, leaves a trace or trail on ourselves; the action is the *karma* and the *samskara* is the trail left behind in consciousness. Once a trail or impression has been made, the *samskara* becomes easier to follow the next time, and the next, like a path through a field. The paths we travel many times over develop deeper grooves, sometimes so ingrained that we may even find ourselves stuck in a rut, wishing to act in one way but now seemingly bound to the trail we've trod so many times before.

In its simplest and most benign form, we can see the workings of *karma* and *samskara* every time we learn a new skill. When my son started walking, the effort and uncertainty was written on his face in every step he took, and he would barely take two steps without holding on to something. Within the space of a month, he was racing up and down the halls. By the time he's an adult, he won't be thinking about walking at all. In fact, as we mature, walking becomes such an unconscious activity that the impulse to take a step forward with the back leg is actually triggered automatically when the front leg lands. In that sense, as we grow up, we have to apply more mental effort to *stop* walking than to keep going. This process of conscious action becoming unconscious pattern is the basic cycle of *karma* and *samskara*, and it plays out from our first faltering steps to our greatest feats of accomplishment.

Karma cuts both ways, though, and while it can clear a path toward growth, it can also dig us into a pit of despair. Giving in to occasional temptation can become addiction, and the resulting *samskara* can leave us seemingly unable to make a turn for the better. Or a traumatic incident can carve a sudden *samskara* so deep that our psyche is transformed in a single moment.

Trailblazing in Your Brain

Yogis developed the notion of *karma* and *samskara* by observing the intricate web of cause and effect that underpins everything we do and who we are. With vastly improved technology, modern neuroscience only recently caught on to what the yogis discovered through introspection alone.

The basic units of your brain are neurons, little multifingered filaments coiled so tightly against each other that in a single cubic millimeter of brain tissue there are four kilometers of neurons. The gap where two neurons meet is called a synapse, and when electricity passes through a neuron, it releases chemicals called neurotransmitters into the gap, where they float across the channel and, depending on the kind of neurotransmitter, they either shut the receiving neuron down or spark a new electrical impulse that travels onward. If you're imagining a few little lights casually flickering on the Christmas tree of your brain, speed it up a bit—this whole process happens anywhere from ten to two hundred times a second. Make the tree a bit bigger, too, because there are about 85 billion neurons tangled up inside you, and since each of them is cozied up against roughly seven thousand neighbors, that means you have about one hundred trillion synapses hanging around in a place where one neuron can say to its neighbor, "Hey, check this out!" or "Shut up over there!" Since each of these connections can either be on or off in a given moment, the number of possible ways you could light up the Christmas tree of your brain is about ten to the millionth power, which is more than the number of stars in the known universe. Turns out Hamlet got it backward: There are actually more things dreamt of in your philosophy than in heaven and earth.

For most of the twentieth century, this is how we assumed your brain worked: you were an embryo and your brain was growing fast, with neurons multiplying over and over every day. You popped out into the world and your brain was still growing, albeit more slowly, but then it was mostly busy learning—forging connections between neurons into reinforced networks. During the critical period of childhood, if you didn't light up something important, like language, it was going to be a lot harder to pick it up later on, maybe even impossible, because as we grow up the brain crystallizes. It gradually stops building new networks, and from there on out you pretty much work with what you've got. Then you get old, and even those networks start to fall apart and can't be repaired, and from that point forward you pretty much spend your time forgetting where your slippers are, playing bingo, and watching *The Price Is Right*.

Here's what's really going on inside your brain: with every thought you think and everything you do, your neural Christmas tree twinkles in a different way. Think of your favorite vacation spot—twinkle. What's 11 x 12?—twinkle. With your left hand, touch each finger to your thumb, one by one back and forth, as fast as you can—twinkle. Every time you do or think those things, the associated neural pathways get stronger. The saying in neuroscience is that "neurons that fire together wire together" by forming neural networks that evolve constantly throughout a lifetime in a process called *neuroplasticity*. The twinklings of your every thought and action become self-reinforcing, and the pattern each lights up in you becomes more ingrained, accessible, and automatic. This is how you learn.

But neuroplasticity is a two-way street—the memory we haven't called up in forever grows fainter, we forget how to solve a quadratic equation after high school, our golf game goes to hell every winter. For many such skills, the brain is a use-it-or-lose-it organ, and established networks that go dormant gradually fade in a process called *synaptic pruning*. Real estate in the brain is a hot commodity, and thoughts and actions we exercise often tend to expand their turf. Meanwhile, if a skill stops using its room in the brain, another skill is likely to move in and redecorate. For example, when a sighted person reads braille, areas of the visual cortex used to see shapes will remain dormant. But while a blind person reads braille, the visual cortex becomes very active, because the brain has rerouted and expanded neural networks associated with touch to fill the space in the brain that sight would normally occupy (Sadato et al. 1998).

Some neural networks come together quickly and are very difficult to undo. Everyday motor skills like riding a bike won't normally be lost without use unless the brain undergoes significant and specific damage. Some basic pattern recognition pathways can be forged almost instantaneously and become nearly impossible to unwire, like an optical illusion that you can't unsee once it's been spotted. In the case of sudden psychological or physical trauma, repeated exposure to threats—or sometimes a single significant incident—can profoundly damage the stress response in both body and brain, leaving sufferers caught in a loop of perpetual hyperarousal or disassociation, which we know as PTSD. These deep networks are all rooted in the unconscious brain, which, you'll recall from the last chapter, acquires patterns and habits very easily but seldom gives them up without difficulty.

The old model of brain development that dominated the first half of the twentieth century isn't entirely wrong. Certain critical periods for learning and developing particular skill sets do exist—language, for example, is much easier to acquire in childhood than in adulthood. And the brain's ability to adapt is itself more adaptable in youth than adulthood. Part of the reason change seems harder as we age is that each new thought and action has to penetrate progressively deeper and denser neural networks accumulated over our lifetime, which means more time and repetition is required to make an impression that lasts. When you're an old dog, there will still be new tricks, they'll just take more practice.

When we're children, everything is new, which means everything is firing and wiring together in brand new ways all the time. We're outside our comfort zone just trying to stand up and say, "Mama." As we age, we can rest a bit more on the laurels of what we've learned, and some of the reason we lose our ability to learn and change so easily is also because we tend to stop *trying* to learn new things when we get old. So don't give up on that dream trip to Paris when you retire—it turns out that trying to learn a new language in adulthood may be one of the best things we can do to maintain our neuroplasticity in old age, precisely because it is so hard (Doidge 2007). Keep the French-English dictionary on your shelf, and stash a good bottle of Bordeaux for your golden years, because you'll be rewiring your brain in big and small ways with every thought and action you take until the day you die. Down to the sparkle in our synapses, we are hardwired for change.

A Meeting of the Minds

If this model of how the brain changes sounds a lot like *karma* and *samskara*, that's because it is. Long before there was any such notion of neuroplasticity or any field called neuroscience, William James, late nineteenth-century philosopher and pioneer of psychology in America, understood the common ground between the ancient idea of *karma* and the modern psychology of habit. While lecturing at Harvard, James met a visiting guest from India, Swami Vivekananda, a renunciate yogi who electrified America's intellectuals a few years prior when his lectures at the 1893 Parliament of World Religions packed auditoriums and newspaper headlines alike. It's no stretch to say that Swami Vivekananda almost single-handedly introduced America to yoga. James was clearly taken with Vivekananda—after their first introduction the two were seen cloistered away in a corner, swapping philosophies well into the night (Bardach 2012). James littered his book *Varieties of Religious Experience* with quotes and concepts borrowed from Vivekananda's most famous works, which expound on the exact practices prescribed in the *Sutras* and the Gita. In his seminal *Principles of Psychology*, James coined a metaphor pulled right from the concept of *samskara* to describe how habitual human nature unfolds the way water, "in flowing, hollows out for itself a channel, which grows broader and deeper; and, after having ceased to flow, it resumes, when it flows again, the path traced by itself before" (1890, 106).

Finally, with advice that might sound right at home coming from Krishna or Patanjali, James leaves us with the following conclusion to his short work entitled *Habit*: "We are spinning our own fates, good or evil, and never to be undone. Every smallest stroke of virtue or of vice leaves its never so little scar" (1914, 67). James echoes Krishna's command to stand up and act, and his conclusion on habit reminds us that while we can't escape its workings, *karma* is not predestination. *Karma* hands us an invitation to take center stage in our own lives, to do what we can to courageously direct our own destiny, and to learn to let the rest go with humility.

The Three Pillars of Transformation

Socrates famously said, "To know the good is to do the good," but I'll risk picking a fight with one of philosophy's heavyweights to say I think Socrates got that one wrong. Maybe he never felt guilty a day in his life, but for those of us who've ever languished in the gap between what we know is good and how we're actually behaving, we're going to need a bit more than knowledge. Take a deep breath and ask yourself, right off the top of your head, "What are three things I should really improve about myself?" I'm going to guess you could've kept going past three. When it comes to what we want to change, most of us know it—or at least tiptoe very near it.

Sometimes, taking action is not the problem, either. We're willing to stand up and fight. Every January is flush with resolve. Every June is littered with would-be changes that never took root. If that sounds like you, don't feel bad: according to one study, more than half of people break their New Year's resolutions within six months, and only 8 percent see them through to success (Norcross et al. 2002). Making change stick is where we stumble, and that's right where Patanjali tries to catch us in the second chapter of the *Yoga Sutras*:

Yogic action requires discipline, self-study, and surrender. (2.1)

Here Patanjali affirms Krishna's emphasis on the necessity of action. Knowing the good is not enough. Reshaping our selves requires belief combined with behavior, and Patanjali encourages three virtues for taking action that will make a difference: discipline, self-study, and surrender.

Discipline

"Discipline" in Sanskrit is *tapas*, which literally means "heat"—such as the heat that comes from friction. *Tapas* allows us to endure the resistance that comes when we go against the grain of habit. When we're in the grip of *samskara*, we need the grit to stay the course when the mountain of our unconscious patterning comes bearing down. *Tapas* is Patanjali's nod to good old-fashioned willpower.

For the study of willpower there's no better scientist than Roy F. Baumeister. If this guy invites you over for an experiment, just say no. Roy Baumeister is famous for doing things like bringing people into his lab with a plate of fresh-baked cookies on the table and telling them they can't have any, then handing them a bowl of radishes to munch on instead. Oh, and then he'll send you next door to work on geometric puzzles that actually have no solution, just to see how long you stick with it. If you were one of the lucky few who got a cookie, you're likely to tinker with the puzzle for about twenty minutes. If you had to choke down a mouthful of radishes, you'll probably tap out after about eight (Baumeister et al. 1998).

Baumeister and his team of tormentors realized that our willpower acts like a muscle and follows two basic principles:

1. You have a finite amount of willpower that becomes depleted as you use it.

2. You use the same stock of willpower for all manner of tasks.

(Baumeister and Tierney 2011, 35)

Like any exercise, we weaken our willpower for a while whenever we use it. Like any muscle, it can be strengthened. Getting enough rest, and eating well so that your brain gets enough glucose (which is what your neurons use for energy) seem to make the biggest difference. Baumeister and his team also found that all kinds of activities could improve willpower—but, interestingly, not all at once: Exercising self-control in one area spread discipline to all areas of life, but when people tried to spread their self-control too thin, everything caved. This suggests we'd do well with our discipline to focus it on one change at a time, so that the friction of our own *tapas* doesn't rub us raw all over.

Self-Study

"Self-study" in Sanskrit is *svadyaya*. In older Hindu traditions, *svadyaya* most commonly referred to the study of sacred sources of wisdom, like the Gita and the *Sutras*. In modern contexts, *svadyaya* evolved to include ourselves as a source of sacred wisdom. *Svadyaya* sends us into the field of our body and mind, like Arjuna, to investigate the truth of our nature and confront the facts of who we really are. Everything in this book, from meditation and contemplation to understanding the contents of your consciousness and the edges of your experience through psychology and neuroscience, are forms of self-study. *Svadyaya* reminds that the path to transformation is personal. Ultimately, we can determine the course of only one happiness—our own—and self-study keeps us constantly listening to our own experience and measuring the impact of our actions in our own lives.

Surrender

"Surrender" comes from the Sanskrit phrase *ishvara pranidhana*. In Hindu religions, surrender is expressed in the form of devotion to God. In the more secular *Yoga Sutras*, surrender shows up in the belief that the transformative experience of stillness, or Self, is out there even though it may seem so strange and distant. *Ishvara pranidhana* keeps us holding to the radical possibility that this moment can be experienced exactly as it is without suffering, while accepting that in any moment we are at play with forces bigger than us and beyond our control.

Patanjali's tools of transformation support each other like the legs of a tripod, and we're bound to wobble when even one is weak. *Tapas* provides the drive to take action in the face of resistance. *Ishvara pranidhana* meets us from the other end with belief that sustains us until those actions take root. All the while, *svadyaya* helps us navigate between the two, discerning when to double-down on discipline and when to let go and accept that we've done all we can for the moment.

INQUIRY: HOLD YOUR BREATH

You can do a little experiment in discipline, self-study, and surrender right now, and you don't even have to put this book down. Hold your breath. Congratulations, you're practicing your discipline. All day long your breath breathes itself involuntarily without you even trying, but look, right now you just chose to stop breathing. All very ordinary and boring, but consider for a moment as you hold your breath that certain mammals like whales and dolphins actually *can't* breathe involuntarily, or they'd drown. So maybe you ought to have enjoyed all that effortless automatic breathing before you stopped, because by now you're probably feeling *something* building up inside you that's pushing back against your discipline.

Study that something. Notice it building. Watch where it starts in your body, how it moves. Notice what it does to your thoughts. What is that something urging you to breathe? Why *can't* you just hold your breath for as long as you want? It may surprise you to find that we actually don't know: researchers have put forth a lot of complex theories involving blood gasses and the phrenic nerve and all kinds of other factors, but when it comes right down to it, the breath you're fighting against taking right now is a medical mystery (Parkes 2006). By the way, how's that going? I bet that *something* is getting stronger. And stronger. And you know, sooner or later (probably sooner), your discipline is done. You'll have no choice but to surrender and breathe. Go ahead. Or if you want to keep going you can take your time. With a little disciplined training and studying a few techniques, most of us will be able to extend our ability quite a bit. But the world record currently stands at about twenty-two minutes, which means no matter how good you get, eventually you'll be surrendering too.

Once you've caught your breath, consider that beyond the meditative goals of the *Sutras*, the tools Patanjali lays out here are instruments that can be used to make *any* kind of transformation empowered and enduring. The principles of discipline, self-study, and surrender pour all our will into the challenge—and keep us honest with ourselves about the things that are beyond our control.

～

Make That Four Pillars…

With all due respect to Patanjali, I'd like to add one more pillar to the architecture of change he lays out in the *Sutras*: compassionate self-acceptance. Compassion has long been a cornerstone in the tradition of Kripalu Yoga, based on the teachings and practices of a renunciate from India named Swami Kripalu, whose name in Sanskrit means "compassionate."

Self-compassion is not at all the same as self-pity, which is a belief that we are victims of circumstance and incapable of moving beyond our situation. In yoga practice, compassion reflects our full commitment to end our own suffering while granting us what my teacher Tal Ben-Shahar calls "permission to be human." Change inevitably starts with a recognition that we are not where we desire to be. Even that recognition is a form of enlightenment. Far from leaving us down in the dumps, self-compassion is what gets us up out of the dirt and into the fight knowing full well that our discipline is limited, that there are corners of consciousness that self-study cannot touch, and that we're seeking something we can't yet fully comprehend.

Compassionate self-regard leads to greater emotional resilience, as well as reduced self-criticism and the ability to more clearly acknowledge one's role in a negative event (Leary et al. 2007). Instead of compounding our suffering with added judgment and criticism, it diffuses further suffering, allowing us to see our own circumstance more clearly and move forward with determination and humility. Moreover, self-compassion correlates highly with key components of change, namely initiative and optimism, as well as happiness itself (Neff, Rude, and Kirkpatrick 2007).

Recognizing the catalytic power of compassion, Patanjali put it atop his list of suitable objects for settling the mind in meditation:

Consciousness calms when one cultivates kindness, compassion, joy and equanimity toward all things, whether good or bad, pleasant or painful. (1.33)

Patanjali harvested these four chestnuts from early Buddhism, where they're known as the *brahmaviharas* or "the four immeasurables"—values and attitudes worth cultivating infinitely toward everything. Compassion in particular is certainly not unique to Patanjali and the Buddha: we can hear its refrain in Christ's command to "Love thy neighbor" and in the Judaic virtue of *chesed*, a compassion central to the goal of *tikkun olam*, or healing the world.

Since compassion is an essential ingredient in so many transformative traditions, it seems worthy of a promotion in our practice too. Patanjali emphasizes cultivating compassion for *everything*, "whether good or bad, pleasant or painful." This practice of radical compassion not only softens the pull of our attachments (*raga*) and aversions (*dvesa*), it also allows us to acknowledge our own shortcomings and dark places without heaping on scorn and creating one more pattern of suffering. It allows us to look the one hundred Kaurava cousins of the Gita—the things that threaten our own heart—right in the eye without sinking down in the dirt.

Substantial evidence suggests that self-compassion can be cultivated and maintained directly through meditation (Hofmann, Grossman, and Hinton 2011; Neff and Germer 2013; Weng et al. 2013). The meditation on self-compassion that follows draws on a traditional Buddhist loving-kindness meditation called *metta*, which we'll expand on later in the chapter on kindness. *Metta* meditation is similar to the concentration meditation we explored in the last chapter, but instead of using the breath as a focal point, we use a *mantra*, which is a phrase of thought repeated throughout the meditation.

INQUIRY: MEDITATION ON SELF-COMPASSION

For this meditation, give yourself fifteen minutes in a place free from distractions. Come to a comfortable seat and allow your eyes to close.

Begin by gathering your attention on your breath, and take a few moments to relax into the feeling of your breath moving itself through your body, all on its own. Let there be nothing else to do right now but breathe and watch and feel.

When you feel ready to continue, shift your attention to your heart in the center of your chest. Imagine that your breath is radiating from your heart to fill your entire body. Allow the inhale to expand in all directions from your center to your edges. Feel the exhale soften and gather around your heart again. Imagine each breath carrying a wave of kindness and gentleness from your heart outward, across your chest and into your arms, down your belly and into your legs, and up toward your head and face. Watch the waves of breath continue, from your heart outward into every single cell in your body. Imagine that every place inside you opens to receive the breath.

When you are ready, bring the following mantra to mind and recite it to yourself as you breathe:

- *May I be happy.*

- *May I be healthy.*

- *May I be free from suffering.*

- *May I be at peace.*

As you recite each phrase, hold yourself in your awareness just as you are right now. With each inhale, imagine drawing the mantra into your heart and spreading it outward to your entire body; and with each exhale return your attention to your heart, then continue with the following breath. Envision that with each breath and each repetition, you are filling more and more with love, kindness, peace, and all the good wishes of the meditation.

Continue the mantra with your breath until the time for your meditation is complete. When you are ready to finish, release the mantra and pause for a moment to notice whatever sensations or emotions remain with you after the meditation is complete. Release that moment with a deep breath, and slowly open your eyes to return to your day.

Be compassionate about your experience of compassion. If this meditation feels forced or awkward in the beginning, that's okay. It's important to remember that you don't have to pretend to feel anything that isn't genuine. It may help to think of the mantra as an offering or an intention for yourself. During this meditation, I often tell students to imagine that each thought is just planting a seed, and there's no need to worry about how it will grow. Just water it with attention and let it be.

Sowing Compassion

With concentration, we taught the mind to sit and stay; with *metta*, we're teaching it to fetch. We learned in the last chapter that conscious thought can contain a tiny amount of information at any time, and from the concepts of *karma* and *samskara*, and the science of neuroplasticity, we discovered that our every thought action is shaping our belief and behavior, creating patterns that will one day become pathways of habit. In this meditation you are literally growing the ability to feel compassion, thought by thought. Meditations like *metta* rely on the limitations of consciousness and turn those limits into a tool for positive transformation. Any moment in which you are occupied with the practice of compassion is a moment in which your consciousness cannot be sowing the seeds of anger, criticism, jealousy, or any of the other negative thoughts and emotions we so often stew in.

This is not a trivial gesture, nor is it an entirely uphill battle. Veteran practitioners with decades of *metta* meditation were able to spontaneously generate genuine feelings of compassion and empathy measured by gamma-wave EEG readings and fMRI activity in the anterior cingulate and insula, in such intensity that they had never before been recorded in research literature (Lutz et al. 2004; Lutz et al. 2008). But those of us who don't have tens of thousands of hours to spare for meditation don't need to worry: a recent study by positive psychology pioneer Barbara Fredrickson documented a seven-week program in loving-kindness meditation that led to significant and lasting gains in self-acceptance, attention, and personal connection, with only fifteen to twenty minutes of meditation five days a week (Fredrickson et al. 2008). A little bit goes a long way.

Inquiry: Questioning Change

Set aside a few moments of *svadyaya* and call to mind something in your life that you would like to change, or perhaps a change you're already in the midst of. What is driving this change? Is it coming from within yourself, or is it driven by external circumstances, or both? What desires and aversions does this change call up in you? Where does it challenge your sense of who you are? What is the best possible result you could imagine from this change? What is the worst outcome?

Where is your *tapas* in this transformation? Is your discipline being spread too thin—are you applying your willpower to many things at one time? Is there one key component to this moment of change where you could focus your *tapas*, even if that means letting some other things go for now?

What elements of this change are outside your control? What are you willing to surrender? Where is your faith during this change—what direction is your compass pointed when doubts emerge? What can you rely on to reinforce your sense of direction when obstacles arise?

Finally, how can you bring compassion to this time of transformation? Are you beating yourself up over the normal and inevitable frictions that change brings? Or are you letting yourself wallow in situations you might actually change? Remember, compassion isn't synonymous with taking it easy. The intent of compassion is to end suffering, which means not only not kicking yourself when you're down but also nudging yourself when you have the power to get up.

An Everyday Superhero

In this chapter, we've seen how ideas from psychology, neuroscience, and yoga come together to illuminate the inevitability of change and highlight how we can harness it in the pursuit of happiness. If you're wondering just how far the tools of meditative introspection we've laid out might take you, this final strange case study in our chapter on change set out to answer exactly that question.

Researchers Robert Levenson and Paul Ekman knew well that meditation could alter the brain in profound ways, but they wanted to test whether meditation's transformative power could reach into the unconscious and primitive territory we normally can't touch. They chose as their test a behavior called the startle response, a defensive reflex we all experience when we're surprised by a sudden, loud noise. This reflex is present at birth and seems to be centered in the brain stem, the oldest of the old neural structures. Their subject: Matthieu Ricard, a Buddhist monk and translator for the Dalai Lama with forty years of meditation experience amounting to well more than ten thousand total hours, including several years spent in solitude. The test worked like this: they'd hook Ricard up to a bunch of gizmos tracking his body, and sometime during the next several minutes a 115-decibel sound—loud as a jackhammer—would suddenly erupt. As far as Levenson and Ekman knew from previous research, the startle response was identical in every individual: elevated heartbeat, increased sweating, and a twitch in five specific facial muscles. Everyone flinched—military sharpshooters, veteran moms of screaming tots, butchers, bakers, candlestick makers—*everyone*. So they hooked up Ricard and set him loose for several different trials including various meditations and just hanging out like a normal guy who wasn't about to have a jackhammer drilling into his eardrum. And guess what happened?

He flinched. I'm sorry—he flinched, he sweated, his heartbeat jumped (Levenson, Ekman, and Ricard 2012). I know, I was bummed too. I wanted meditation to make us all into superheroes. But c'mon, what'd you really expect? This is the *brain stem* we're talking about—it doesn't get any more automatic than that. To be fair, Ricard's reaction was drastically and impressively reduced to a degree beyond any other individual they'd encountered, especially during a kind of meditation called mindfulness, which we'll explore in the next chapter. But in the most basic way, he reacted like us all. We should know by now that while meditation holds out an extraordinary promise, that promise is to make us fully human—not superhuman. And sometimes humans flinch.

Time to Hit the Highway

In the first part of this book, we kicked the tires on the human condition quite a bit. The mind in particular looks like quite a bit of a fixer-upper. Conscious attention doesn't have a ton of horsepower, and the steering swerves us toward suffering at the slightest bump. But with yoga, meditation, and positive psychology, we've also found some incredible tools in the trunk, and some world-class mechanics have hitched a ride with us. With a lot of elbow grease, this jalopy might just start to purr again.

The second part of this book takes us on a journey through the landscape of our lives, from deep within to the world around us, from present to past and future and back again. Along the way, we'll deepen the practices we've been cultivating here and add new ones at every stop. Buckle up. This is where the rubber meets the road.

PART II

THE JOURNEY

CHAPTER 5

Now:
Look

Now is the time to understand more, so that we may fear less.

—Marie Curie, scientist

I once heard a joke in a meditation class that if you ever need to hide something precious, the best place to stash it is in the present moment. Because nobody ever looks there. I know, it's a terrible, terrible joke. Meditators aren't exactly known for their comedy. Still, there's a lot of truth in the punchline. Many of us spend nearly half our waking hours with a wandering mind, boarding trains of thought that circle the same repetitive, negative tracks and never seem to let us off in a happy place. Neuroscientist and longtime meditator Sam Harris sums up our situation nicely: "For most of us, thinking is like being kidnapped by the most boring person on earth and being told the same story over and over again." After a while, we develop a bit of Stockholm syndrome and start identifying with our captor.

This chapter is about staging a rescue and bringing attention home to the present moment. We'll build on the meditation practices we've culti-vated so far to venture even further inward, then dive right back into the world to discover the ingredients for deep engagement with the activities of daily life. Because what good is insight if you can only find it sitting still?

Mindfulness Meditation

In chapter 3, we taught the mind to sit still by giving it the focus of the breath to chew on. In the previous chapter, we taught it to fetch with the meditation of self-compassion. Both forms of meditation are rooted in concentration. Now we build toward a new kind of meditation known as mindfulness. In concentration, we say to the mind, "just look at *this*," whereas in mindfulness meditation, we say to the mind, "*just look.*" Mindfulness meditation originated in a Buddhist practice called *vipassana* and became popular in the West through the work of Jon Kabat-Zinn and his mindfulness-based stress reduction (MBSR) programs, taught in eight-week seminars at medical centers worldwide. Because the MBSR program was standardized and developed with the medical field in mind, mindfulness also happens to be one of the most widely researched meditation forms, and it offers an array of benefits. In numerous reviews spanning hundreds of trials and thousands of participants, mindfulness has been found effective in relieving anxiety, depression, stress, and chronic pain (Grossman et al. 2004; Goyal et al. 2014). In some cases, mindfulness meditation proved as effective as traditional cognitive behavioral therapy and drugs (Khoury et al. 2013). On the up side, mindfulness has been shown to increase attention span, reduce emotional reactivity, and contribute directly to subjective well-being (Keng, Smoski, and Robins 2011).

As Kabat-Zinn describes it, "Mindfulness is awareness, cultivated by paying attention in a sustained and particular way: on purpose, in the present moment, and non-judgmentally," (2012, 1). Mindfulness meditation holds awareness in a slightly different way than the concentration meditations we've been exploring. Rather than focusing on a single object such as the breath, in mindfulness we watch whatever sensations, thoughts, and feelings arise naturally, without letting the mind get caught up in following or directing any one thing.

Mindfulness practice often starts with elements of focused attention to calm the body and remove distractions, and then follows with a gradual releasing of the effort required to sustain a singular focus. Even the task of concentration is allowed to fall away—as the popular Buddhist saying goes, in mindfulness, "There is nothing to do, nowhere to go, and no one to be." In this state of effortless attention, meditation offers us a chance to watch the ebb and flow of thought and sensation, without resisting or adding anything.

~~~~~~

INQUIRY: MINDFULNESS MEDITATION

Give yourself fifteen minutes in a time and place free from distraction. Take a comfortable seat that allows you to sit tall without becoming rigid, to be alert but relaxed. Let your hands rest on your knees or in your lap. This time, let your eyes remain open but with a soft, unfocused gaze—it may help to settle your eyes on the empty space a few feet in front of your nose.

Allow yourself to become aware of the space around you, and let sensations from the outside world come to you—sounds from the environment, the feel and smell of the air, and the image presenting itself to your vision. You don't have to look or listen for anything at all. Just notice whatever comes to you. If it helps, remind yourself, "There is nothing to do, nowhere to go, and no one to be."

Now allow your attention to relax into your body. Feel the weight of your body, its subtle movements, and its contact with the surface beneath you or the air around you. Now let your attention relax deeper into your breath. Allow the breath to breathe itself, as much as you can, in and out through your nose. Feel it rising and falling in the belly or chest. Hear its sound. Feel the sensations at the nostrils and upper lip, where breath enters and leaves the body. Follow one breath into the next, and give yourself a few moments to let attention settle into the experience of breath. Let this tide of effortless breath become a place you can return to anytime.

As time passes, a sensation in the body may become stronger than the feeling of your breath. Let your awareness release the breath and notice this sensation. Be with this sensation for as long as it naturally holds your attention. Watch this new sensation as it evolves, notice its shifting and changing, just as you watched the ebb and flow of your breath before. When the sensation no longer holds your attention, let it go, and return to your breath.

Sometimes a sound will draw your awareness out into the world. Let the breath go and listen. Notice its volume, its distance, and its texture. Be with the sound for as long as it carries your attention, and when attention naturally subsides, let the sound go. Return to your breath.

When a thought or emotion arises, let your attention move to what is present there. Feel what is happening. Where is this thought or emotion felt in your body? When attention touches a thought or feeling, does it change? If you notice that the mind has become lost in thought, or that a feeling has a strong hold on your focus, give it a name or a label. "This is remembering... This is fear... This is pain." Or simply, "Thinking... Feeling..." Sometimes in simply naming thoughts and feelings, they naturally recede from awareness; sometimes they continue.

Greet new sensations, thoughts, and feelings with a friendly curiosity. Notice everything that offers itself to your attention. There is nothing to push away and nothing to hold on to. You can choose to return to the breath at any time.

Let this process continue until your time for meditation is complete. Return to the breath one final time. Notice what has changed. Notice feelings or thoughts that have emerged or are lingering. Finish by offering yourself a moment of compassion and kindness. Thank yourself for the awareness you have brought to your own experience and for everything that experience has brought to your awareness.

Itching to Do Something

In meditation, certain thoughts or sensations may grab hold of the mind and whisk it away before you even notice. It may start with something small—an itch on your nose, which brings an impulse to scratch, maybe even a twitch of your hand, all so fast that it happens before you even have a sense of having made a choice or had a conscious thought at all. This is not unusual, but wherever and however the impulse begins, at some point we catch it. Sooner or later, we become aware of where the mind is at. In that instant a choice arises: Do you let your mind have that feeling or do you let that feeling have your mind? What happens if you don't scratch? What happens if you just watch the itch? Does it have the same pull as time passes—does it intensify or soften? Does it move or change? Does it kick up other impulses or thoughts? A little itch can tickle just about every aversion and attachment you've got; it can make you think you're going to die, if you let it. Or you can just watch. Or you can just scratch. Remember, all our inquiry is built on the bedrock of self-compassion. The last thing we want is for mindfulness to become some kind of medieval trial by ordeal. So sometimes we scratch.

When there's a distraction you can't just watch, deal with it and then come back to watching. I know of no one who has ever said, "Well, I was almost enlightened, but then I itched my nose, so I guess I'll have to wait another lifetime." At the same time, don't sell yourself short. Be willing to be surprised by your ability to just look at the present moment, without having to do anything about it. In mindfulness, everything receives your awareness, but only some things will require your action. Figuring out whether this is the moment to double down on your discipline or surrender to a sensation you simply cannot sit with can be an illuminating exercise all its own.

The Waves and the Witness

When you find yourself in a moment where there is nothing to do or fix or change, when you truly observe the pull of thoughts and feelings arising, when you can watch without having to follow along or resist, something unique emerges. In the meditation, when you noticed your thoughts wander, what part of you noticed the wandering? It couldn't have been your thoughts—they were somewhere else. When you brought attention back, *who* brought it back? A gap has opened in the waves of thoughts, and we must admit that there is something in consciousness that is *not* thought, something in us that *watches* thought.

This watching experience pulls back the curtain on one of meditation's most important and transformative insights: *You are not your thoughts.* When all else we have known is a mind constantly in motion, what else could we be but the sum of thoughts and experiences in this body over time? But in a moment of stillness, as we learn to watch the waves and return to that watching place again and again, we begin to see that thoughts themselves are simply objects of a deeper awareness beneath the ebb and flow of everyday thinking.

In Kripalu Yoga, we call this watcher of thoughts *witness consciousness*, or simply the witness. An experience of the witness may be fleeting at first—so fleeting in fact that the noticing may itself be enough to renew the ripples of motion in the mind, and the witness seems to disappear inside the waves once more. But when we return to the meditative moment repeatedly, we find that the witness is simply obscured by the current of thought, not dissolved. In moments when the movement of thought ebbs, the witness sees itself seeing, and through repeated visits we come to realize that this part of us is always present, all the time.

The Witness in the Lab

This all may sound like a far-out philosophical idea, but neuroscientists have found provocative evidence of something like the witness in the folds and firings of the brain. Using an fMRI to monitor neural activity, a team of researchers at the University of Toronto measured the neural activity of everyday people and trained mindfulness meditators as they explored two distinct states of consciousness: *narrative focus*, following trains of thought about oneself over time, and *experiential focus*, holding attention solely in the present moment. Narrative focus revealed a high activity in the medial prefrontal cortex (mPFC), an area that typically lights up when our minds are wandering in thought (Farb et al. 2007). In fact, this area is active so regularly that it is part of what's called the brain's resting state or *default network* (Gusnard et al. 2001). Think about that for a moment: you don't have to turn the lights on in the part of your brain that tells you stories about yourself, because you basically leave them on all the time. Your father would be so annoyed at you for wasting energy.

By contrast, moments of experiential focus in the present revealed diminished activity in the mPFC in both everyday people and experienced meditators, but the difference in meditators was more pronounced (Farb et al. 2007; Brewer et al. 2011). This suggests that something fundamentally different happens in the brain when we simply watch the present moment rather than follow the wave of thoughts away from the here and now, and that meditation can indeed alter the biology that allows us to be present.

The same study found that experiential focus engaged a brain area known as the right insula, which plays a key role in monitoring all of our bodily sensations and generating emotions connected to those sensations. This is where it gets interesting: for everyday folks, activity in the insula wires together with activity in the mPFC—the exact area involved in following thoughts and creating narrative focus. For most of us, the part of our brain that just watches sensations is tangled up with the part that starts telling stories about those sensations. The two areas functionally lock together, which means that, by default, most of us *can't* experience the present moment without simultaneously tying it into the narrative of past and future.

Except for the meditators. In moments of experiential focus such as mindfulness meditation, as trained meditators witnessed sensations, they increased activity in the insula without automatically triggering the mPFC to generate thoughts and stories about those sensations. The study concludes by suggesting that the minds of meditators "may represent a return to the neural origins of identity, in which self-awareness arises from the integration of basic [...] bodily sensory processes. In contrast, the narrative mode of self-reference may represent an overlearned mode of information processing that has become automatic through practice" (Farb et al. 2007, 320). Meditators were able to separate sensation from story, and in doing so they altered one of the most basic habits of the human mind. They had broken the tie between the witness and the waves.

The Anatomy of Identity

Noted neuroscientist Antonio Damasio traces a similar distinction in the anatomy of our brains between what he calls *core consciousness* and *extended consciousness* (1999). Core consciousness, similar to experiential focus or witness consciousness, consists of a nonverbal awareness of oneself rooted in the present, generated moment to moment in the act of engaging with the world. Extended consciousness, like narrative focus, builds on core consciousness to expand our sense of self beyond the present moment and connect the feeling of being to memories of the past and anticipations of the future.

We can see evidence that both these mental behaviors—a core consciousness of feeling like "me right now" and an extended consciousness of feeling like "me over time"—rely on separate brain structures when we look at what happens when either goes missing. For example, in epileptics with absence seizures, a brief interruption of core consciousness leaves the epileptic appearing temporarily without any presence in the moment or memory of the event once it has passed. Since the experience of past and future is built on the back of a multiplicity of moment-to-moment experiences, when core consciousness collapses it inevitably takes extended consciousness down with it. It's difficult to even imagine someone with only narrative consciousness: a full capacity to remember his or her past and imagine the future, but absolutely no here-and-now experience of the present moment. History offers no such cases.

At the other end of the spectrum—someone stuck completely in the present with no conscious access to the past and future—we have lots of examples. Damasio offers the phenomenon of transient global amnesia, a temporary condition often connected to migraine headaches in which a person loses all memory of his or her past and thoughts of the future, while retaining full awareness of the present moment. In such cases, core consciousness has been retained while extended consciousness has been lost (1999).

From Many Streams, One Current

The concepts of witness consciousness, experiential focus, and core consciousness are not identical, but they share a recognition that everyday experience is not the result of a singular, unified consciousness. There is no master in the machine. Instead, experience emerges among multiple layers of consciousness—separate threads of self that interweave and often tug at one another to create the seemingly smooth experience of "me" and "now." Patanjali agrees wholeheartedly and connects this seeming smoothness of the self to a familiar source of suffering:

Asmita is what makes consciousness appear individualized.

Multiple consciousnesses, each with its distinct activity, seem to gather into one. (4.4–5)

Asmita, you may recall from the roots of suffering in chapter 2, is the innate human tendency to bundle every experience into the story of "me" and to carry that sense of "I-am-ness" like a pack on your back through the years. Patanjali singles out *asmita* as the aspect of the mind that not only gives us a sense of self but also obscures our true nature, which is actually built on multiple simultaneous streams of experience merged together and made to look like a single thing called "me." A full understanding of consciousness may never be possible, and much of the mind remains impervious to the tools of science and philosophy. Even so, it's impressive that Patanjali (with a lot less gadgetry and knowledge than we have access to today), arrived at an insight that most modern neuroscientists agree on: that pretty little package you think of as "you" is actually constantly coming apart at the seams.

Letting Go of Stories

Mindfulness quiets this self-making, narrative aspect of consciousness so a deeper, often unnoticed awareness can take center stage for a while. It's a way to see beyond our stories, and the yogis found something essential worth seeing in there. This may be where some part of you steps in to object, "But I *like* my stories. My memories are important to me, and if I can't think of the future how I am I supposed to get anything done all day? Clearly you have not seen my awesome vacation photos or my huge to-do list." And you'd be totally right about that. Happiness is deeply intertwined with our relationship to the past and future, and anyone who tries to talk you out of that relationship is selling you short. The extreme case of transient global amnesia highlights how essential the storytelling self really is. Without it, we'd all just be wandering around in circles bumping into each other over and over again saying, "Nice to meet you."

But the studies we've just seen and, more important, the wealth of our own experience, suggest that over a lifetime our storyteller gets such a workout that most of us can't *stop*, even if we tried. And having a story-teller that can't shut up has the unfortunate consequence of creating a lot of suffering when reality constantly keeps doing things that don't agree with the story we keep telling. The problem, Patanjali points out, is that we are living as if the present moment exists to give us more stories. But we've got it backward—our storytelling ability exists to lead us back to the present moment:

Now, this is the inquiry of Yoga.

Yoga stills the movement of consciousness.

Then the Self appears in its essence.

Otherwise, the movements of consciousness appear to be the Self.
(1.1–4)

Patanjali lays it all out right from the very first word. *Now.* Yoga, the discovery of our most essential Self, can only happen *now*, because if the mind is focused anywhere else, we are lost in thought. Thoughts seem like a special part of our identity because they appear to arise from within rather than beyond the body's borders, but Patanjali believes that thoughts and things are made of the same stuff. While the idea may initially seem absurd, consider that every single thing you are physically sensing right now is the result of material interactions that are translated into the electrical firings of your brain. The feeling of this book in your hands is not happening in your hands, it's happening in your mind. A thought is the exact same process. Patanjali would argue that a thought is no less material than the sound of a ticking clock, and the sight of a passing cloud no more material than a memory. We are not so separate as we seem. If we can succeed in tracing any of these things back to their source, they reveal the same simple underlying witness.

When we remain with that witness, there is a kind of freedom to be had. Unpleasant thoughts can be seen as any other object. No effort needs to be made in suppressing or banishing them—they can be felt fully and observed to pass naturally. This does not mean painful things cease to be painful, or that we walk around in constant bliss. It simply means we can experience pain as pain without having to add insult to the injury. Pleasant moments do not need to be clung to or collected or inserted into the storybook of who we are. While we can't always live in that mindful space, when we're there, we are free to experience the moment completely as it is. In doing so, we become a little less a creature of reactive habits and a little more a being built on conscious choice.

This is why when the mind becomes lost in thought, in mindfulness meditation we may label the contents of a moment simply by saying, "This is warmth" or "This is pain" or even just "Thinking... Feeling..." There's no need to add any "I" to the experience, such as "I am warm... I am thinking." In effect, we're cutting off narrative focus by concluding the story succinctly without adding extra chatter. In doing so, we're free to come back to witness the present moment, exactly as it is. We begin to see things as they are. That's the heart of mindfulness and yoga: *the experience of now, with nothing to add.*

Insight in Action

As sweet as that may sound, all the mindfulness and meditation we can muster will take us only so far sitting on our butts. While Patanjali whispers in one ear for us to embrace the present moment in stillness, we've got Krishna in the other telling us to get up and make a move. And if the *kleshas* just come pouring down as soon as we stand up, we're in trouble.

William James, the pioneering psychologist and fan of Swami Vivekananda we met in the third chapter, hinted at this dilemma in *The Varieties of Religious Experience.* In that book he sought to plumb the depths of what he called the mystical experience, which he describes as an altered state of consciousness that defies language and reveals a depth of knowledge beyond everyday awareness:

> *Our normal waking consciousness, rational consciousness as we call it, is but one special type of consciousness, whilst all about it, parted from it by the filmiest of screens, there lie potential forms of consciousness entirely different. We may go through life without suspecting their existence; but apply the requisite stimulus, and at a touch they are there in all their completeness.* (1985, 373–74)

James collected reports of all kinds of mystic experiences, from the ecstasy of prayer to the awe of nature to the intoxication of alcohol. He found such uncanny consistency in these stories of altered consciousness that he believed they pointed to deeper psychological truths.

Yet later in the same passage, James himself confesses that he only came to this determined revelation about consciousness after huffing a bunch of laughing gas. Which simply highlights the problem: if the only way to set aside our stories and access the joy of deeper awareness is to sit down and close our eyes to the world, or get high on nitrous oxide, what is to become of daily life? How can we rise to action as Krishna commands without sinking into a world of suffering at the first step? Can we experience selfless awareness and still keep our day job? James had no answer to these kinds of questions, but he expressed keenly both the transformative potential of a mystical moment and its pitfalls, pointing to the long history of mystics that had fallen away from society, and, in James's own 1900 America, even into insane asylums.

In the 1960s, psychologist Abraham Maslow grabbed the baton James held out and ran with it. His pioneering work on *peak experiences* looked beyond James's focus on religious visions, meditation, and intoxication and into the lives of ordinary people engaging with the day-to-day world. He found twenty-five common characteristics of peak experiences, including many things that may ring a bell to an experienced meditator: a dilation of time, a vividness of perception, and the sense of self falling away to reveal an underlying unified awareness (Maslow 1964). Moreover, he found that these were normal and essential human moments, found in the lives of everyday people just as much as religious believers and spiritual seekers— sometimes even more so. Maslow's work took the foundations of a mystical moment out of the hands of religion and offered it to everyone:

> *I can go so far as to say that this intrinsic core-experience is a meeting ground… for priests and atheists… for artists and scientists, for men and for women… for athletes and for poets, for thinkers and for doers… All people have or can have peak-experiences.* (1964, 58)

As we're about to discover, peak experiences don't always require us to step back from the world. They can be found just as well when we jump in feet first.

Going with the Flow

I imagine that if Krishna ever met Mihaly Csikszentmihalyi, he would probably kiss him square on the face. A psychologist hunting for the heights of human experience in the tradition of Abraham Maslow and William James, Csikszentmihalyi first became fascinated by artists so deeply engrossed in their work that they would forsake food and sleep without any apparent consideration. His early work on what happens when we become absorbed in action soon spread to every corner of the globe, encompassing dozens of studies and thousands of participants. Csikszentmihalyi and his colleagues scrutinized neurosurgeons, champion chess players, Japanese motorcycle gangs, Detroit steelworkers, and just about everyone in between to uncover a universal quality of experience underlying moments when we are feeling our best while doing our best (1990). He called this underlying experience *flow*.

The Criteria for Flow

Mihaly Csikszentmihalyi found that everyone can experience flow and that it relies on just a few basic principles (Nakamura and Csikszentmihalyi 2009):

- **Intense concentration on the present moment:** The ability to focus, and to focus *only on the relevant information*, is the single greatest determinant of a flow experience. We have seen the circumscribed capacities of consciousness, and if attention is constantly divided and distracted it cuts us off from the opportunity for absorption. Without a capacity to focus, the engaging frontiers of flow are impossible to reach. See, aren't you glad you've been meditating since chapter 3?

- **Clear goals and immediate feedback:** To find a flow state we have to know where we're going. Without an objective or a sense of direction, effort and attention have no place to be applied. And unless we can tell whether we're scoring points or landing the steps or making the right moves, we'll get lost along the way. Sports and games are inherently engaging in part because they are structured to let us know what to aim for, and because they tell us how we're doing as we go. Goals and feedback in flow activities aren't always explicit to the outside observer, but they're intuitive and immediate to the experiencer. For example, if you've ever stayed up into the wee hours thrilled by a captivating conversation, you may wonder if that could count as flow. Certainly—the goal may be bonding and personal connection, and the feedback comes with all the subtle emotional cues that come as you open your heart and mind to another human being.

- **Challenges that match your skills:** Flow happens at the sweet spot where your abilities match the action *exactly*. Too much challenge and you'll be anxious, too little and you'll be bored. Consider that the next time you're on your yoga mat, straining to wrap your leg around your head. If your focus is frantic and your breath is ragged, it's a good sign that you're pushing past a place of potential flow. On the other hand, if you can recite everything on your grocery list, you may want to kick it up a notch. For flow to flourish, you need a challenge meaningful enough that everything in you *has* to come together, but manageable enough that it *can*.

The Experience of Flow

What do we get in exchange for all this effort and attention? Quite a lot, it turns out.

- **A loss of narrative self-consciousness:** There is little or no awareness of oneself.

- **The merging of action and awareness:** Attention is completely absorbed by the activity.

- **A sense of knowing precisely what to do:** Everything is in the right place at the right time.

- **Time feels altered:** These are the moments when the minutes last for hours and the hours fly by.

- **The activity becomes an end unto itself:** The action is intrinsically rewarding, whether or not the goal is reached.

Where Did I Go?

Notice how closely the experience of flow lines up with the inward experience of meditation, particularly the loss of narrative self-consciousness. People in flow routinely report that they are so engaged by whatever activity is at hand that their sense of self diminishes or disappears. They say, "I forgot I was even there," or "It was like I wasn't even the one doing it." Not surprising, self-transcending flow states correlate with decreased activity in the medial prefrontal cortex, or mPFC (Peifer 2012), which is a little chunk of brain you may recall from the experiment on narrative focus and the storytelling self by Farb and friends (2007).

The overall effect, known as *transient hypofrontality* (which literally means "there's temporarily not a lot going on up front in your brain"), is theorized to be the unifying neurological principle beneath both meditation and flow (Dietrich 2003, 2004). In flow, as our precious conscious resources are poured completely and wholeheartedly into action, sense of self dissolves, and awareness merges with the activity. It's as if we *become* the action.

Compare that to Patanjali's description of a moment of full meditative absorption known as *samapatti* or "falling together":

As waves in consciousness still, it becomes transparent like a jewel,

and doer, doing, and done coincide as one. (1.41)

Or Krishna from the Gita:

One who has known the truth thinks, "I am not the doer,"

whether seeing, hearing, touching, smelling, eating, walking, sleeping, breathing. (5.8)

Though meditation sends us traveling inward toward stillness while flow sends us out into action, we may be surprised to arrive, if not at the very same address, then at the least in a strikingly similar neighborhood.

The dissolution of the ego in flow can serve as a powerful antidote to *asmita*, the suffering that arises when we try to protect our sense of self. We've seen how things that threaten the familiar story of "me" often trigger strong aversions and touch on deep *samskaras*. Yet paradoxically, in flow I feel most fully alive in a moment when there is no "I" to be found. Such a moment must give us pause, at least to wonder whether this "I" we have been so carefully crafting really requires such constant guarding and maintenance.

When the sense of self we forsook for flow finally comes home again, it returns transformed. We have traveled beyond the edges of our familiar selves, and, as Csikszentmihalyi describes it, when the borders close again the territory has expanded:

During the long watches of the night the solitary sailor begins to feel the boat is an extension of himself, moving to the same rhythms toward a common goal. The violinist, wrapped in the stream of sound she helps to create, feels as if she is part of the "harmony of the spheres." The climber, focusing all her attention on the small irregularities of the rock wall that will have to support her weight safely, speaks of the sense of kinship that develops between fingers and rock, between the frail body and the context of stone, sky, and wind...

One could treat these testimonials as poetic metaphors and leave them at that. But it is important to realize that they refer to experiences that are just as real as being hungry, or as concrete as bumping into a wall. There is nothing mysterious or mystical about them. When a person invests all her psychic energy into an interaction—whether it is with another person, a boat, a mountain or a piece of music—she becomes a part of a system of action greater than what the individual self had been before. (1990, 64–65)

Transformation is hardwired into flow experiences. We thrust the entirety of our consciousness into an action and, in doing so, prime our brains for change. From the perspective of yoga, actions in flow create deeper *samskaras* and shape ourselves in ways much more profound than passing thoughts or daily routines. If you've ever been in an accident, you know how time seems to expand and the moment becomes branded in memory. The same arousal processes in the brain that distort time, memory, and learning during life-threatening situations are also present in flow. But unlike the scars of trauma, repeated flow experiences can engender positive and enduring self-concepts and behaviors that change our lives for the better. As of yet, we have no clinical name to describe the transformative growth that may come from peak experiences like flow. Positive psychologist Tal Ben-Shahar suggests "post-peak-experience order" as a counterpoint to the concept of posttraumatic stress disorder. Krishna might call it a kind of enlightenment.

INQUIRY: FINDING FLOW

Set aside a few minutes to explore where you find flow in your own life. Do you have a favorite flow activity? When was the last time you felt so deeply engaged in what you were doing that your sense of self fell away?

Are there places where you once found flow that have slid into boredom? Places where you were once immersed that now leave you feeling anxious? What might you do to raise the bar or hone your skills in those activities?

Dedicate ten minutes to writing about a particularly vivid flow experience. Don't try to analyze it or understand why, just relive its glory. Describe the sights and sensations, the flashbulbs of memories that linger from the moment, perhaps the insights that have endured, and how the moment changed your sense of self.

~~~~~~~

Uprooting Suffering

Both the Gita and the *Sutras* hold out the possibility that through disciplined and compassionate inquiry, in time any moment can be witnessed without suffering. It seems like an incomprehensibly faraway vantage point. Experiences of mindfulness and flow serve as reminders that the enlightenment we are seeking is not a distant destination but something that exists right now—in fact, it can *only* exist now.

Mindfulness and flow both ground us in the present and lead to self-transcending experiences of the here and now. Whether embodying the moment in stillness or in action, we arrive at a place where *asmita*—the familiar story of the self—begins to dissolve. When we uproot any one of the *kleshas*, they all begin to whither. As the story of "me" subsides, clinging *raga* has less to hold on to. Pushy *dvesa* loses its leverage. The fog of *avidya* lifts a little. The haunting *abhinivesa* that rises at the thought of my inevitable dissolution (a tough one "even for the wise," Patanjali comforts us) may even feel a little less frightening. I can see that "I" am not so permanent and not so separate. And it's not so scary.

Meditation teacher Michael Stone writes that "If the self is fictional and not a static and eternal entity, we can begin to embrace it as such" (2008, 89). He links that embrace to a beautiful quote from poet Wallace Stevens: "The final belief is to believe in a fiction, which you know to be a fiction, there being nothing else. The exquisite truth is to know that it is a fiction and that you believe it willingly" (1957, 189). In the next chapter, we'll explore that "exquisite truth" and embrace the self wholeheartedly again with the yogic concept of *dharma*.

CHAPTER 6

Dharma:
Look Within

A self is made, not given. It is a creative and active process of attending a life that must be heard, shaped, seen, said aloud into the world.

—Barbara Myerhoff, anthropologist

Back on the battlefield of the Bhagavad Gita where we first encountered yoga, Arjuna is more confused than ever. Krishna has been going on and on about the infinite value of spiritual wisdom, encouraging Arjuna to seek out his true Self, and warning him about the pitfalls of worldly pursuits. When you're staring down a sharp and pointy wall of bloodthirsty relatives, so far it's not exactly the most rousing pep talk.

"Krishna," he complains, "If you keep saying that knowledge is better than action, why do you keep telling me to stand up and fight?"

Arjuna's confusion makes total sense in the context of our own journey up until now. Patanjali called us inward to still the waves of the mind, shedding layer upon layer of illusions about ourselves along the way. Krishna seems to jump on board with that plan in the Gita by saying that yoga is "equanimity of awareness" (2.48), only to turn right around and tell us that yoga is actually "skillfulness in action" (2.50). So what *is* yoga? Patanjali's still mind or Krishna's excellent action? Wisdom or work? *Both*, is Krishna's bold reply:

Fools speak of a divide between knowledge and action, but the wise do not.

Travel either path truly, and you reap the harvest of both.

True knowledge and skillful action are fruits of the same tree.

To see the Self at the heart of knowledge and the center of action is to truly see. (5.4–5)

Krishna makes a brief nod to separate paths for both knowledge and for action, then blows Arjuna's whole question wide open by pointing out that you can't have one without the other. None of us are exempt from the turnings of the mind or the inevitability of action. We are on both roads, all the time, and yoga is the process of learning to tread evenly with one foot in wisdom and one foot in work, which the Gita calls *dharma*.

Wisdom at Work

The Gita's very first line opens with all the warriors gathering on "the field of *dharma*" (1.1). When Arjuna loses his nerve, he's literally collapsing into the dirt of *dharma*; as a metaphor, it's the ground for Krishna's entire instruction. It's also one of yoga philosophy's most complicated concepts—a puzzle that starts with just figuring out what *dharma* means, because it has no easy English translation.

The *Sanskrit* root of "*dharma*" is "*dhri*," which means "to support or hold up." In some of its earliest appearances it referred to the laws governing the universe—the natural laws that held up the cosmos from chaos. If you traced the word through time, you'd see its meaning gather focus from the infinite to the individual. *Dharma* gradually came to be applied to the principles that support the functioning of societies, then families, and by the time our hero sinks down alone in the field of *dharma*, it's clear that we're here to discuss what to do with the life of just one person: Arjuna—who's really only holding the spot in the story for you.

Pick up a dozen different copies of the Bhagavad Gita, and you'd most often see *dharma* translated as "duty," which resides in the neighborhood of what Krishna is getting at but doesn't quite hit home. For most of us, duty calls up images of being commanded, or doing what someone else expects of us—whether it's our family or our job or our religion or our culture. The *dharma* Krishna describes is not that at all: when Arjuna asks why he should fight, Krishna doesn't bend down to bark a cosmic "because I told you so" in his face. Instead, he says to Arjuna:

If you cling to your sense of self and think, "I will not fight,"

your determination will be useless, and your nature will thrust you into action.

Your own karma, born of your nature and bound by your actions,

will drive to do the very thing you decide in delusion not to do.
(18.59–60)

Dharma in the Gita is ultimately a force from within, not from without. Krishna is intimating that there is something in Arjuna, and in each of us, driving us to the metaphorical fight, and he connects it to our *karma*. Remember though: *karma* is not fate or predestination. Certainly, some of Arjuna's *karma* was handed to him at birth, just as each of us is constrained by what the genetic lottery has dealt to us and shaped by forces of environment and culture we may never fully understand or influence.

We also shape our own *karma* by how we play the hand we're dealt, and the Gita is calling us to take an active role in upholding and supporting the unfolding of our own lives. Doing so requires an ability to understand what we're really made of and the determination to use what we've been given to the utmost. The tools of discipline, study, and surrender that Patanjali encourages us to take up will serve us well on the field of *dharma*. In that sense, we might land closer to what Krishna is talking about by thinking of *dharma* as "inner duty," a path inextricably intertwined with the world outside but ultimately and intimately unique to each of us.

Better to Struggle in Your Own Dharma

While Arjuna is still wrapping his head around the mess he's gotten into, Krishna drops a bit of a bombshell into their chat.

Better to struggle in your own dharma than to succeed in another's.

Better to die doing your duty, for the path of another is fraught with fear. (3.35)

For me, understanding *dharma* through Arjuna's eyes shed a new light on my story from the start of this book, so many years before, when I got called for the academic opportunity of a lifetime…then put down the phone and puked. Throughout college I had pursued majors in both theater and economics, trying my best to straddle love and levelheadedness. If I was being honest at the time (which I wasn't), the whole economics degree was basically a front for doing what I most enjoyed, which was telling stories about what it means to be human. I practically lived in the university's theater building—a dusty old renovated church building caked with paint and pockmarked with nail holes from thousands of tales that had been told and put to bed long before I ever set foot on the stage.

Many nights I slept in the space, and I easily spent twice as much time there as in class. I did every conceivable job—sets and costumes, lighting and props—but most often I was an actor. During the course of that collegiate career, I was strangled to death on six occasions, shot twenty-two times (twice on Saturdays), and received eight stab wounds. I dished it out as much as I took it, though, and slept with several men's wives (and one wife's man), demolished a Greek village with an earthquake, and became King of England. What can I say? It was a legendary time. But it was also drawing to a close with my impending graduation. Like all my peers, I was facing down the prospect of getting a real job in the real world, and the economics degree standing in the background was suddenly thrust into the spotlight.

It wasn't that I didn't like economics—I did, in a way. My specialty was game theory—a field of economics made famous by John Nash, a brilliant thinker whose battle with paranoid schizophrenia was chronicled in the book and film *A Beautiful Mind*. Game theory deals with strategic decision-making: how people interact and compete in groups and games. It's a math-heavy discipline with applications that stretch into nearly every corner of human behavior, from economics to politics to biology to philosophy. I still have a particularly vivid memory of sitting in one early-morning class pondering equations so dense and sprawling that they covered chalkboards on three full walls of the room. Navigating the labyrinth of signs and symbols, guided by an impulse honed with years of study, I suddenly stopped short at the center of it all, gazing in awe of the secret language of numbers whispering before me. I felt as if I were being allowed to peek behind the curtain of the universe. It was a moment of flow as pure as I'd ever known, though I had no clue to call it that at the time. Yet, while it was a thrilling perk of the academic lifestyle, it was also an all-too-rare part of the average day job in my field. What I saw out there involved little of the mysteries of the universe and a lot of staplers and spreadsheets.

Flash-forward to the night I got the call from the British consulate, and all my *karma* was coming home to roost. I had spent years impersonating a passionate young student of economics, and those actions had rippled out and brought back fruit that should have been the sweetest I'd ever tasted. For four solid years, I'd tried to cram my thumping heart into this square and straitlaced career path. It just wouldn't fit. My heart wasn't in it. And in the end, it didn't matter that it was the smart choice. It didn't matter that saying yes would open a door that had turned many others into Nobel Prize winners, even presidents. What mattered, in the end, was that something deep in me spoke out and said, "*Stop.* Just stop. This is not your life."

Joseph Campbell put it beautifully, as he usually does: "You must give up the life you planned in order to have the life that is waiting for you." I didn't have his maturity and eloquence, so I threw up instead. But the message got through all the same. The body I thought was betraying me was actually calling out a warning that it would take me years to fully understand. I had been seeking success in a *dharma* that wasn't mine, and that path was becoming fraught with fear.

In my case, the important factor wasn't whether I had skill or enough challenge. If I had said yes to economics, there would have been abundant challenges ahead that would test and grow that skill with moments of flow that might make standing in that circle of chalkboards as I had done in class seem like child's play. But for flow to open a doorway to *dharma*, we need more than just skill and challenge. Those skills have to touch on the core of who we are, and the challenges have to put that core into action.

For Arjuna, that core is as a warrior prince. Again and again, Krishna reminds Arjuna that his duty is to fight for what is right and protect his kingdom.

> *Do not waver in the face of your duty.*
>
> *For a warrior, there is no higher calling than to fight for what is right.*
>
> *Warriors given a chance like this are blessed with an open door to heaven,*
>
> *and should be happy to encounter such a battle.* (2.31–32)

To open the doorway to our own *dharma*, first we need to understand our own character.

Patanjali's Yamas and Niyamas

The cultivation of character is central to the project of yoga. In the eight-limbed pathway of self-discovery laid out in the *Yoga Sutras*, Patanjali dedicates the first two limbs to questions of character, called the *yamas* and the *niyamas*. In Sanskrit, *yama* means "restraint," and the five *yamas* are ethical observances that regulate our relationship to the world around us, while the five *niyamas* are personal virtues that regulate our relationship to our inner world.

The Yamas

Ahimsa: nonviolence

Satya: truthfulness

Asteya: non-stealing

Brahmacharya: managing energy, avoiding distraction

Aparigraha: non-grasping or possessiveness

The Niyamas

Saucha: cleanliness of mind and body

Santosha: contentment

Tapas: self-discipline

Svadyaya: self-study

Ishvara pranidhana: surrender

You'll recognize three of the *niyamas*—discipline, study, and surrender—as the pillars of transformation highlighted in the fourth chapter. Patanjali gives that trio of traits an extra nod, but he suggests in the *Sutras* that if you're aiming to get a good look at your Self, you'd do well to call upon all of them as you shape your self.

All of the *yamas* and *niyamas* are already present in you. These are not quirks of the genetic lottery, like perfect pitch or height, whereby you either luck into it or lose out. The *yamas* and *niyamas* are indwelling aspects of ourselves that we either choose to cultivate through action or let wither with neglect. Like every action, they carry *karma* that reshapes our sense of self. But in this case Patanjali singles them out because their *karma* leads toward the stilling of consciousness that illuminates the Self. These are important attributes for Patanjali's journey inward, but what should we consider cultivating for a journey out into the world?

Values in Action

The history of happiness beyond Patanjali's *Yoga Sutras* overflows with collections of character traits that have been said to open the doorway to heaven, as Krishna so colorfully put it. The Buddha offered up the *brahmaviharas* of loving-kindness, compassion, altruism, and equanimity. Aristotle and Plato singled out temperance, justice, courage, and wisdom as the four to count on in the pursuit of self-realization. Christianity tacked on an additional three with faith, hope, and love to form the seven central virtues (1 Corinthians 13:13). Benjamin Franklin cooked up a list of thirteen virtues that looked a lot like Patanjali's—including sincerity, moderation, and cleanliness. He famously tried to master them all by rotating throughout the list and conquering one each week, though he confessed in his autobiography that while he felt better for the endeavor all in all, he missed the mark more often than not ([1818] 2010).

Scratch beneath the surface of any philosophy or religion, and we're sure to find some set of values or virtues meant to empower our actions and steer our work in the world. How to choose? Inspired by that very question, founding father of positive psychology Martin Seligman teamed up with researcher Christopher Peterson in search of the character strengths that are common to humanity across time and culture. They pored over the texts and tradition we've just been talking about among hundreds of others—everything from the Koran to the Klingon code, the Boy Scouts of America to the Bushido samurai. Ultimately, they settled on six core virtues that span three thousand years of history and serve as an umbrella for twenty-four character strengths that pop up again and again in the pursuit of happiness (Seligman and Peterson 2004):

The VIA Classification of Character Strengths and Virtues

1. Wisdom and Knowledge

Creativity: Thinking of novel and productive ways to conceptualize and do things; includes artistic achievement but is not limited to it.

Curiosity: Taking an interest in ongoing experience for its own sake; finding subjects and topics fascinating; exploring and discovering.

Judgment: Thinking things through and examining them from all sides; being able to change one's mind in light of evidence; weighing all evidence fairly.

Love of Learning: Mastering new skills, topics, and bodies of knowledge, whether on one's own or formally.

Perspective: Being able to provide wise counsel to others; having ways of looking at the world that make sense to oneself and to other people.

2. Courage

Bravery: Not shrinking from threat, challenge, difficulty, or pain; speaking up for what is right even if there is opposition; acting on convictions even if unpopular.

Perseverance: Finishing what one starts; persisting in a course of action in spite of obstacles; "getting it out the door"; taking pleasure in completing tasks.

Honesty: Speaking the truth but more broadly presenting oneself in a genuine way; taking responsibility for one's feelings and actions.

Zest: Approaching life with excitement and energy; not doing things halfway or halfheartedly; living life as an adventure.

3. Humanity

Love: Valuing close relations with others, in particular those in which sharing and caring are reciprocated; being close to people.

Kindness: Doing favors and good deeds for others; helping them; taking care of them.

Social Intelligence: Being aware of the motives and feelings of other people and oneself; knowing what to do to fit into different social situations; knowing what makes other people tick.

4. Justice

Teamwork: Working well as a member of a group or team; being loyal to the group; doing one's share.

Fairness: Treating all people justly; not letting personal feelings bias decisions about others; giving everyone a fair chance.

Leadership: Encouraging a group of which one is a member to get things done and, at the same time, maintaining good relations within the group.

5. Temperance

Forgiveness: Forgiving those who have done wrong; accepting the shortcomings of others; giving people a second chance; not being vengeful.

Humility: Letting one's accomplishments speak for themselves; not regarding oneself as more special than one is.

Prudence: Being careful about one's choices; not taking undue risks; not saying or doing things that might later be regretted.

Self-Regulation: Being disciplined; controlling one's appetites and emotions.

6. Transcendence

Appreciation of Beauty and Excellence: Noticing and appreciating beauty, excellence, and/or skilled performance in various domains of life, from nature to art to mathematics to science to everyday experience.

Gratitude: Being aware of and thankful for the good things that happen; taking time to express thanks.

Hope: Expecting the best in the future and working to achieve it; believing that a good future is something that can be brought about.

Humor: Liking to laugh and tease; bringing smiles to other people; seeing the light side; making jokes.

Spirituality: Having coherent beliefs about the higher purpose and meaning of the universe; knowing where one fits within the larger scheme; having beliefs about the meaning of life that shape conduct and provide comfort.

INQUIRY: YOUR SIGNATURE STRENGTHS

Take a peek at the list of character strengths Seligman and Peterson have compiled. As you scan the list, notice three or four strengths that strike you as central to who you are. If you'd like to take it a step further, you can complete a free survey offered online by the VIA Institute on Character at http://www.viacharacter.org/www/The-Survey, or just notice which traits reach out and grab you.

Seligman hypothesizes that each of us has several *signature strengths*—traits that feel essential to who we are that we yearn to apply and find joy in cultivating in many different domains (2002). What are your signature strengths? Once you hone in on a handful that feel central to you, can you think of defining moments in your life when those strengths emerged?

Keep It Personal

The great thing about Seligman and Peterson's list of values is not that it's exhaustive or authoritative—far from it. Remember, they set out looking for the character traits that were held in high regard throughout all time and culture. However, you only have to do your living here and now. Which means that if you look at Seligman and Peterson's list and think they missed a real gem of a strength that's precious for you, or if you took their survey and didn't find a value that you know fits you like a glove, then *trust yourself*. The same is true for Patanjali's *yamas* and *niyamas*. Patanjali was writing for people almost two thousand years ago who never had to deal with the joys of the thirty-year mortgage or the perils of online dating. It's foolish to think that he and we have nothing in common, but it's just as foolish to fetishize a few lines from an ancient author who may not have even existed. Deciding upon and defending what you value is an essential part of *dharma*, and if you delegate it, then it becomes one more story, one more construct that stands between you and the Self. If we're just getting our values off a list from the *Yoga Sutras* or a research report, we're in trouble. At the end of the day, that's not too far removed from a *Cosmo* quiz.

Instead, lists like these serve us best as a springboard from which you can dive into an inquiry on the traits that are essential in your life. It's tempting to look at Seligman and Peterson's character strengths and leap right to the places where we feel we're lacking, or make a plan to mend our perceived shortcomings. For my part, I have never ranked highly on bravery. I've taken Seligman's inventory dozens of times over a decade, and every single time, bravery cowers limply at the bottom of my list. Should I go out looking for bar fights to break up, or burning buildings stocked with rescueable kittens and babies? Seligman suggests that there's another way to mine the territory of our character, and it starts not by dredging up flaws but by digging into the soil that's already fertile and building on the signature strengths found there (2002).

～～～

INQUIRY: SKILLFULNESS IN ACTION

Take a moment to recall one of your absolute favorite moments of flow. Think about an activity in which you felt fully alive and totally engaged. If you haven't already, complete the journaling exercise Finding Flow from the previous chapter with this activity in mind.

Now, ask yourself what character strengths this activity called upon, cultivated, or challenged. For instance, writing is (on a good day) a flow activity for me, and when it's really humming it taps in to my love of learning as I research and gather material, challenges my creativity and perseverance as I lay everything down on the page, and even sparks my sense of social intelligence and love of beauty as I tinker for the perfect phrase or the right image to light up an idea.

And don't worry about matching the strengths involved in your flow experience to the VIA list or to Patanjali's yamas and niyamas. This is a chance for you to explore what's at work underneath an activity essential to your being, so you can give whatever name you like to the signature strengths that emerge. Gather those strengths into their own list.

With those signature strengths as a foundation, expand your attention further into your life. Are there other things you do that call upon the same qualities? Are there activities you might alter in such a way as to cultivate your signature strengths? Others you might take up? Trace these qualities of character through as many defining moments of your life as you can find, and see where the threads lead you.

Following Your Bliss

When we find flow activities that draw upon our signature strengths, we're knocking on the doorway of *dharma*. When a flow experience taps in to something vibrant and vital within us, it offers that essence an expression through action. Because a signature strength reflects an aspect of character that is already highly cultivated in us, it is by its nature an ideal ingredient for deep flow experiences, which thrive on the confluence of extraordinary skills matched with great challenges. The strength alone is insufficient, and letting it languish in the background is a waste of potential that brings no bliss. But when we put our signature strengths into action, they are strongly tied to a greater sense of well-being, less stress, and increased positive affect (Linley et al. 2010; Wood et al. 2011). Here, Krishna, the philosophers, and the psychologists all concur: when we come to understand the nature of the self, and we act in ways that exercise and express our unique and essential selves, it makes us happy.

Too often we fixate on the specifics of the action and miss the indwelling strengths it's meant to express. For example, from a very young age, I loved snorkeling. I was Jacques Cousteau waiting to happen. The first time my parents let me loose in the ocean was during a short stop on a cruise, and I was so captivated that I didn't notice I'd drifted far beyond the beach until hours later when they had to haul me out of the water after much panicked searching. That summer, the twelve-year-old who couldn't stop looking at starfish told everyone who would listen that he was going to be a marine biologist. I had no clue what that career really entailed, but I assumed dolphins would be involved.

For years, I had this pining in the background of my brain to return to the reefs. Then I gradually discovered that submerged beneath the hobby of diving was a curiosity and a love of beauty that was constantly trying to bubble up to the surface. What I needed more than the ocean was to give the curiosity and appreciation an outlet. I started collecting rocks and minerals, learning about stars, building models—suddenly there were sources of absorption and amazement just about everywhere. That same fascination with the world outside later led me inward to the study of psychology and the deeper practices of yoga we're exploring here. Once we've got ahold of a signature strength, opportunities for action may spring up in abundance.

Again, I can count on Joseph Campbell to lay out so clearly a pathway I only stumbled upon:

> If you follow your bliss, you put yourself on a kind of track that has been there all the while, waiting for you, and the life that you ought to be living is the one you are living. Wherever you are—if you are following your bliss, you are enjoying that refreshment, that life within you, all the time. (Campbell and Moyers 1991, 142)

It sounds so simple and lovely and suitable for framing. But what most people don't know is that Campbell came to this conclusion directly from the same ideas we've been studying with Patanjali and Krishna in search of the Self. When the yogis went seeking the Self, they didn't try to approach it from the front by guessing at what the Self is; instead they set out to strip away everything the Self *isn't*. Whatever couldn't survive the scrutiny of their meditations couldn't possibly be the essential, enduring Self. Under the power of their inquiries, almost everything crumbled—the external world, the senses, the thoughts, the mind, the ego, and on and on—until only three attributes of Self remained that could not be stripped away. They captured that essence in the Sanskrit phrase: *satchitananda*. Campbell describes the meaning of *satchitananda* and how it led to his focus on bliss:

> *The word "Sat" means being. "Chit" means consciousness. "Ananda" means bliss or rapture. I thought, "I don't know whether my consciousness is proper consciousness or not; I don't know whether what I know of my being is my proper being or not; but I do know where my rapture is. So let me hang on to rapture, and that will bring me both my consciousness and my being."* (Campbell and Moyers 1991, 149)

The Sanskrit phrase *satchitananda* tells us that we will know the Self by three things: being, consciousness, and bliss. Throughout this entire book, we've been exploring the convoluted corners of the mind and searching for clues to the tricky question of who we really are. Campbell acknowledges that it's a jungle in there. His genius was to suggest that rather than heading straight into the tangled thickets of our own thoughts and grappling with the existential uncertainties of metaphysics, we might just as well grab ahold of the one thing we can know without a doubt when we're in its presence: bliss.

"Follow your bliss" is easily Joseph Campbell's most oft-repeated quote and the one that has buoyed up a whole armada of quick-fix self-help solutions for what to do with your life. But keeping up with bliss takes *work*. We're committing to a radical reorganization of the self in service of the Self. We are not signing on to be carried by the hand, limp and dangling. The bliss that Campbell describes, the flow Csikszentmihalyi found, and the *dharma* offered up in the Gita are not external forces that will let you coast along in their wake; they are internal drives that will not let you rest until you have offered them into the world through action.

From that perspective, we'd be better served by thinking less about how to follow our bliss and more about how to carry that bliss with us and bring it to everything we do. Having seen so many people latch on to his quote expecting an easy and effortless ride, Campbell himself was reputed to mutter late in life, "I should have said, 'follow your blisters.'"

From self to Self and Back Again

Through the first half of this book, we trailed Krishna and Patanjali inward, searching for the Self beyond passing thoughts and everyday experience. Whatever you ultimately discover while spelunking in your own soul, the Gita offers a clear reminder that it's impossible to stay put in there forever.

> *Nothing in the world purifies like true wisdom;*
>
> *time and practice will reveal the Self within you.*
>
> . . .
>
> *With the sword of wisdom, cut free the doubt and illusion in your heart,*
>
> *Then arise and follow the path of action, Arjuna!* (4.38, 42)

Dharma describes the necessary journey back out into the world of work and love and pleasures and pains, and the only way back from the Self leads through the very same self we came in on. But it's not the same ride heading back. Krishna suggests that the process of Self-discovery changes how we handle the self. Having shed our stories, even for a moment, we grow to appreciate not only the limitations and pitfalls of the self but also its unique strengths and characteristic quirks carved from a lifetime of *karma* and *samskara*. Better understanding our own nature leads toward a pursuit of happiness built around expressing those strengths and passions in action. How those actions touch the people around us is the topic of the next chapter.

CHAPTER 7

Connection:
Look Around

If you want to make others happy, practice compassion.
If you want to be happy, practice compassion.

—Dalai Lama XIV

You have to learn to love yourself first before you can love someone else. This particular platitude makes the rounds in self-help and spirituality circles so often that we might just nod and pass it on without a second thought. In one of her many best sellers, *What I Know for Sure*, Oprah Winfrey writes that "life is a journey of learning to love yourself first, then extending that love to others" (2000, 31). If Oprah knows it for sure, then it's gotta be true, right? Get your self-love sorted out, and you'll have all you need to give to others—it just sounds so intuitive.

The yoga tradition approaches the whole concept of compassion from a very different angle. Imagine you were to head out right now and toss yourself on the doorstep of an ashram, pleading, "My life is empty of love, all I can see is suffering, and none of my scented candles smell good anymore. Help me!" You know what your first step on the road to rediscovered bliss and unconditional love is likely to be? Chores. Come on in and chop vegetables. Stay the night and scrub the floor. In communities built around the practice of yoga and meditation, selfless service, or *seva*, is a basic foundation for spiritual growth and liberation from suffering.

Don't know how to love yourself? No problem, say the yogis, you can start by learning to love others. Having trouble finding happiness within? Help someone else find his or hers. The concept of *seva* puts a provocative kink in the me-first mentality that bliss must begin within, and this chapter answers that challenge by exploring the happiness that can be found in serving the people around you. In the Gita, Krishna puts the question to Arjuna quite plainly:

> *In a spirit of selfless service anyone can reach enlightenment.*

> *Without the spirit to serve, Arjuna, how could one be happy here or anywhere?* (4.31)

A Two-Way Street

Lest you read on thinking I'd dare to dis Oprah in print, let me be clear that I don't think she's wrong about love. Healthy self-love absolutely improves the love we give to others. The very real need for self-love is a big reason why we dedicated a considerable part of chapter 4 to cultivating self-compassion. Later in this chapter, we'll go about extending that compassion to others, exactly as Oprah prescribes.

But when we tell ourselves that our self-love has to be complete before it can support another's, or when we believe our own happiness must necessarily come first, we create a chronology of well-being that causes as many problems as it solves. There is no day in which you will suddenly awake to find that, at last, you love yourself completely. There is no single step that will finally land you in happiness. These are constantly evolving inner relationships that have no endpoint. If we keep on reciting the mantra that we have to learn to care for ourselves first, our compassion for others withers on the vine waiting for an idealized moment that will never arise. Self-love undoubtedly improves the love we spread, but the opposite can be just as true.

In a seminal study on more than 2,500 volunteers, Peggy Thoits and Lyndi Hewitt tracked how service impacted six measures of well-being: happiness, life satisfaction, self-esteem, sense of control over life, physical health, and depression (2001). Their results were clear and convincing: volunteer work matched with better outcomes on every single measurement, and those improvements scaled with the number of hours served. In and of itself, this came as no great surprise—the correlation between volunteerism and well-being is longstanding. The real question lies in whether greater well-being made people volunteer, or whether the service improved their well-being. After all, it could be the case that happy people naturally tend to volunteer more, just as Oprah foretold. To determine which was really the cause and which was the effect required a longitudinal study, like Thoits and Hewitt's, to follow volunteers over a long period of time. So which way does the arrow point?

Both. Volunteering improved well-being, and positive well-being made one much more likely to volunteer, creating a mutually reinforcing spiral (Thoits and Hewitt 2001). The circle runs both ways, and we can step in at any point, meaning that we actually don't need to wait until we feel good to lend a hand. In fact, those in poor well-being may benefit most of all from serving others (Piliavin and Siegl 2007). Sometimes, helping others helps us most when we ourselves are most in need.

This is not to say that serving others provides a substitute for the necessity of self-care. All of us have moments when we are overextended in helping others and need to carve out dedicated time and resources for ourselves. And the debilitating phenomenon of burnout among volunteers, caregivers, and helping professionals is well documented (Maslach, Schaufeli, and Leiter 2001; Maslach 2003). Service sustains us best when in balance, and it's not a panacea. But it's not simply a reserve that empties from one person to another, leaving you depleted as you fill your neighbor's cup. The actual relationship between helping and happiness is much more intricate and much more rewarding.

Altruism

"Altruism"—the ability to place the well-being of others over oneself—was coined by Auguste Comte in 1830 as the opposite of what he called "egoism," a self-centeredness of the kind that Krishna and Patanjali have been warning us about for quite a while now. And the spirit of service Krishna encourages may be innate. At Germany's Max Planck Institute, psychologists Felix Warneken and Michael Tomasello set up a lab in which they videotaped toddlers playing alone. They watched how the children responded when an unfamiliar adult dropped something and couldn't reach it. In their lab, kids as young as eighteen months typically stopped what they were doing in order to help a stranger in need (2006).

Kindness of this sort may not only be innate but intuitive as well. Researchers at Harvard and Yale found that when subjects were given a small sum of money and then offered a chance to donate part of what they'd been given, they gave away significantly less when encouraged to think about their decision; they were much more generous when giving was spontaneous rather than deliberate (Rand, Greene, and Nowak 2012).

While Comte placed altruism and egoism at opposite ends of the spectrum, in the brain they are deeply intertwined. Serving others triggers neural activity in reward centers such as the nucleus accumbens, the same basic areas that light up when we ourselves experience the pleasures of food or sex or money (Harbaugh, Mayr, and Burghart 2007). And while we're on the subject of money, research led by Elizabeth Dunn showed that people who spent money on others were typically happier than those who spent the same amount on themselves (Dunn, Aknin, and Norton 2008). What I give to you turns around and transforms me as well.

When her colleague Laura Aknin later wanted to extend the same inquiry to children, she had to change the rules of the game a little and substitute snacks for money. (Which makes perfect sense to me: When my two-year-old was given a crisp new hundred dollar bill for his birthday to start a savings account with, he tried to put it in the toilet; when he has a box of raisins, he thinks he's royalty.) So Aknin and her team gave kids a pile of treats to snack on and then invited them to give some away to a colorful puppet. Sure enough, the kids expressed the most delight when sharing (Aknin, Hamlin, and Dunn 2012). Together, Aknin and Dunn's research on giving demonstrates the same self-reinforcing circle we found earlier in volunteers: giving makes us happier, and the happier we are, the more we give.

The Case Against Having a Full Cup

Lest we protest that the happiness of Aknin's and Dunn's research subjects may have arisen from having enough of their own resources to take pleasure in the privilege of giving some away, data from 136 countries, including a multitude of impoverished communities, shows that giving routinely makes us happy (Aknin et al. 2013). Our cup really doesn't have to be full to give, and those who are emptiest are often sharing the most. In America, the poorest fifth of the population donates more than twice as much of its income to charities—3.2 percent—compared to the wealthiest fifth, which donates only 1.3 percent (Stern 2013). That trend is only widening: a 2012 report by the Chronicle of Philanthropy found that from 2006 to 2012, the wealthiest Americans reduced their giving by 4.6 percent, while in the same period, middle- and lower-income Americans upped their charitable contributions by 4.5 percent (Daniels 2014).

The argument could easily be made that the absolute dollar amount given by affluent donors far eclipses that of the less wealthy, but on the other side of that argument lies the fact that for poorer donors, each extra dollar donated actually extracts a greater cost as a percentage of their total income compared to the wealthy. For the poor, the stakes are higher, and yet they give more. The bottom line is that in spite of the high-profile philanthropy of a handful of billionaires like Bill Gates and Warren Buffett, altruism seems to thrive most in everyday people at the bottom of the heap.

Generosity in the Lab

The go-to measure of generosity research is a totally unfair and wildly boring game called The Dictator Game. Imagine you're plopped into an empty room and told that you're about to play a game with an anonymous partner who you will never see or encounter again. The princely sum of $20 is up for grabs, and by the flip of a coin, all the loot goes to lucky you. Before you head out to tell your friends that you just struck it rich, you're invited to give as much or as little as you choose to your invisible partner.

What would you do? A pure egoist would take the money and run. On the other hand, you only ended up with that twenty bucks thanks to the flip of a coin, and in the other room, you imagine a less-fortunate soul who's just been told, "Thanks for coming in—now please go home, loser." In practice, most people don't walk away with all twenty bucks, even when the game is set up so that the subject knows that nobody—neither the researchers nor his or her "partner"—is watching. Research on tens of thousands of would-be dictators across diverse cultures has been offered up as evidence that, in our heart of hearts, we are not solely selfish creatures (Henrich et al. 2004).

Before we go patting ourselves on the back, though, let's consider some other ways this game has been played that don't make us look quite so beneficent. Imagine now that you're plopped down in a similarly bland and empty room and told that both you and your invisible partner have both been given the (less) princely sum of $10. By the flip of a coin you become the "dictator." Raw power surges through your veins. Before you leave, you may choose to give some of your money to your partner or walk away as before, but now you also have the option to *take* some of their money. What do you do? Since you're reading a chapter on kindness and compassion, I am willing to bet there is a tiny voice inside you saying, "I think I'd give at least a little." But I'm also willing to bet there's another, louder voice inside you right now that knows exactly how this game usually ends. I'm sorry to say, that voice has it right. When the dictator game expands to include the possibility of taking, most of us usually snatch a little something from our neighbor's pile before heading for the exit (List 2007; Bardsley 2008). Generally, we're not total jerks: most people leave their invisible partner with at least a few dollars. Enough for a bummer of a bus ride home. Absolute power may not corrupt absolutely, but it doesn't make us very generous at all.

A research team led by Paul Piff at the University of California, Berkeley decided to take the game a step further by first measuring participants' socioeconomic status to note, as we might expect by now, that poorer participants give away more in a traditional dictator game than their wealthier counterparts (Piff et al. 2010). In a later experiment, they tweaked subjects' sense of social status before having them complete a survey on how people ought to spend their salary, including questions targeting what percentage someone ought to give to charity. Subjects made to feel better off suggested giving significantly *lower* than those made to feel worse off than others (2010).

If you're not already feeling sufficiently pessimistic about the relationship between social status and altruism, Paul Piff will gladly squash your hopes a little more: Through the course of seven separate experiments, he and his colleagues found that as we scale the social ladder we become increasingly prone to lie, cheat, and steal (Piff et al. 2012). For example, in one of those studies they sat at California crosswalks, where the law mandates that drivers must stop for pedestrians waiting to cross. They counted not only how many cars broke the law but also what kind of cars. The oldest and cheapest cars stopped every single time, but the more expensive the car, the more likely it was to breeze right through and break the law while leaving pedestrians waiting in the dust. (Apparently, BMWs were the worst, so next time you see one rolling up to you on the street, I'd get out of the way if I were you.) As startling as that study's conclusion may seem, in terms of overall blunt messaging, nothing really tops Piff's experiment that put participants in a waiting room with a bowl of candy on the table and then told them that the candy was for children in a separate study taking place simultaneously. You can see where this one is going: people higher up the social ladder proved more likely to literally take candy from children.

Too Stressed to Care

If it's true that we're born to be kind, then how do we possibly descend from innate compassion to stealing candy from kids and running down little old ladies in the street? Stress plays a major role, and it takes no great scientist or philosopher to realize that when we're under pressure, none of us behave in the most benevolent ways. Consider how many humbled apologies you have heard (or given) that started with some variation on the phrase, "I'm sorry, I've just been really stressed out..." That clichéd admission harbors a surprising degree of truth. In chapter 4, we outlined the major biological pathway for stress, starting in our old friend the amygdala, which sends a distress signal to the hypothalamus, triggering a chain reaction from the anterior pituitary gland down to the adrenal glands, which then dump the hormones adrenaline and cortisol into the bloodstream. Once we're surfing on a wave of cortisol, our whole organism shifts toward the priority of self-preservation; there's little room left for consciousness to consider taking care of others.

Consider this humbling experiment conducted by two of the leading psychologists studying altruism, Daniel Batson and John Darley, at Princeton University. They gathered a bunch of the school's theology students and told each of them that they were about to give a talk on a religious topic. Some of the students were told that they would be speaking on the topic of Jesus's Good Samaritan parable—the Bible's central story about helping those in need no matter who they are—while others were given a variety of unrelated topics. Then they told everyone that their talk would take place in another building, that they would be given no time to prepare, and, to up the ante, they told some of them that they were already late, so they'd better hurry. Along the way, researchers had staged the route so that each student would pass by a man slumped over, coughing and groaning. All in all, more than forty students encountered the apparently suffering man. While we'd all like to believe that if we walked by someone in need *while thinking about how important it is to help people in need* we'd stop to help, that's not actually what happened. People who were preparing to speak about the Good Samaritan were no more likely to stop than people thinking about any other topic. The only thing that made a difference was whether they felt like they were in a hurry (Darley and Batson 1973). Being in a hurry raised the theologians' stress levels and narrowed their focus, and they walked right on by, even when the object of their story lay groaning at their feet.

Cortisol—the so-called "stress hormone"—often comes off looking like the bad guy when it comes to compassion, but it actually plays a vital role: while too much cortisol pulls us into a largely automatic and self-centered focus on survival, too little not only leaves us unable to respond to genuine threats to ourselves but also unmoved when we encounter suffering in others. Low levels of cortisol are associated with a lack of empathy and, in extreme cases, even psychopathy (Shirtcliff et al. 2009). We actually need the stress hormone to get compassion off the ground. But if we can't regulate our own response to the feeling of stress, then cortisol floods the engine and the whole endeavor of compassion comes crashing down. Research has shown that people who are better at managing their own emotions and less prone to spikes in emotional volatility (both positive and negative) respond to others in more compassionate and empathetic ways (Eisenberg et al. 1994). When emotions are running high, those who cannot consciously intervene and redirect the unconscious stress response find their capacity for compassion dwindling.

Without the critical capacity for self-regulation, every stressful moment hijacks our attention, and we become more and more stuck within ourselves. The tools of meditation we've been cultivating throughout this book help us to keep our hand on the steering wheel and to regain control quickly when surprises come our way. Abundant evidence suggests that meditations of concentration and mindfulness improve the capacity for attention and emotional regulation (Davidson et al. 2003; Feldman et al. 2007; Tang et al. 2007). Some research even hints that prolonged meditation is associated with diminished activation of the amygdala both in and out of the meditative state, suggesting that meditation dials back the stress response before the cascade even begins and creates enduring changes in our brains (Lutz, Slagter, and Dunne et al. 2008; Desbordes et al. 2012). In meditation, we don't dispel the emotions, but we don't let them take over. You still get to have the feelings, the feelings just don't get to have you. And that leaves you freer to see beyond yourself and into others.

When Love Is in Your Veins

If cortisol is often the biological culprit when compassion collapses, then another hormone deserves special mention when it flourishes. Oxytocin, sometimes cutely referred to as the "cuddle hormone," is created in the hypothalamus and stored in the posterior pituitary gland. You may recall that these little nuggets of neural anatomy play key roles in the stress response; it so happens they're also vital to the expression of love and compassion. While the pituitary stores hormones to help you freak out in the front, it also stocks hormones to help you snuggle up in the back. Oxytocin mediates all kinds of social behaviors, from simple social recognition and mother-child bonding (it's released in abundance after birth) to increasing trust between people (Carter 1998; Kosfeld et al. 2005). In certain circumstances, oxytocin also diminishes amygdala activity in association with fear, and it appears to inhibit or regulate the familiar fight-or-flight response to stress (Kirsch et al. 2005; Huber, Veinante, and Stoop 2005). Sure enough, along with a diminished stress response, oxytocin also makes us more kind and generous (Zak, Stanton, and Ahmadi 2007). In place of the fight-or-flight response, the presence of oxytocin during times of stress tends to stimulate social behaviors like nurturing others and creating and cultivating social networks—a phenomenon dubbed the "tend and befriend" response by the researchers who first studied it (Taylor et al. 2000). All in all, this sweet little molecule seems like the key to compassion, and we should all like a little more of it, right?

But just like there's a bright side to cortisol's role in compassion, the cuddle hormone has a darker side as well. The warm glow of oxytocin may not shine equally in all directions. People given oxytocin in the lab do indeed demonstrate a spike in all kinds of compassionate social behavior, but that behavior seems to stop right at the edge of one's familiar social circle. Beyond those boundaries, helping behavior quickly fades, and increased levels of oxytocin actually amplify defensive and noncooperative behaviors against people perceived as outsiders. The brain's response to oxytocin may be less "tend and befriend" and more "tend and defend" (De Dreu et al. 2010; De Dreu 2012). While oxytocin lights us up in the company of loved ones, it also gives us a serious case of stranger danger. Where we draw the edge of our circle of friends has a major effect on just how far our compassion can actually spread.

The Other

The tendency to favor the people we perceive to be like us and to treat them better as a result, often by punishing outsiders, is called *in-group bias*.

It's a phenomenon writ large by Shakespeare in the tragedy of *Romeo and Juliet*, but we all enact it every day in big and small ways, contributing to everything from major social problems like racism and sexism to things as subtle and silly as who yawns when you yawn (Campbell and deWaal 2011). Studies of in-group bias generally focus on clearly defined social markers like gender, race, and class, but the group you're "in" doesn't even have to mean anything to set this bias ablaze. In a famous series of experiments, British psychologist Henri Tajfel and colleagues divided people into groups in a way that was obviously arbitrary, completely anonymous, and utterly inconsequential, only to discover that, even when the line in the sand is totally meaningless, we'll still be kinder to the people standing on our side (Tajfel et al. 1971).

Many psychologists at the time hypothesized that our propensity for in-group bias resulted naturally from competition over scarce resources, but Tajfel's genius was to demonstrate that we behave in a way that disregards those who are different even without the specter of scarcity looming over us. In Tajfel's experiments, there was nothing over which to compete, and he hypothesized that competition only exacerbates an even deeper tendency to rely on our membership in various groups as a means of constructing and maintaining a sense of stable identity. We use in-group bias to reflectively reinforce our own self-esteem, often to the detriment of others and, paradoxically, sometimes even to ourselves (Tajfel 2010).

Dr. Seuss made a satire of this bias in his story of the Star-Bellied Sneetches, who discriminate against their bare-bellied brethren until a man comes to town and offers the plain Sneetches a chance to use a machine that will give them a star on their bellies for the low, low price of three dollars, only to turn around and offer the original Star-Bellied Sneetches a trip through another machine for ten bucks to remove their stars. As Sneetches scurry from one machine to the next, the identity crisis escalates "until neither the Plain nor the Star-Bellies knew. Whether this one was that one or that one was this one. Or which one was what one or what one was who" ([1961] 2006, 10). In the end, the man packs up and leaves behind a gaggle of penniless Sneetches to reflect on their folly.

The Maintenance Cost of the Ego

Here we begin to see the shadow cast by the ego in stark relief. Paul Piff suggests that in-group bias explains part of the phenomenon of dwindling benevolence alongside rising wealth that his team found in the candy-takers and lawbreakers (Piff et al. 2012). If we accrue resources only to self-segregate into similarly well-off independent groups, then we encounter the suffering of others less and less by comparison and become less dependent on others to address the struggles in our own lives. The result may be a diminished capacity for altruism. Data from a 2012 study at the Chronicle of Philanthropy revealed this dynamic playing out in cities and towns across America: nationwide, the average level of charitable contributions for families earning more than $200,000 was 4.2 percent. When a similar family lived in a zip code where more than 40 percent of their neighbors were also making more than $200,000, giving dropped to 2.8 percent (Daniels 2014). When all we see all day are people like us, and when it looks like those people are doing just fine, then where's the reason to lend a hand?

This evaporation of compassion has serious consequences beyond dollars and cents and tax deductions. In one study, psychologist Dennis Krebs asked people to observe others playing a roulette game. He led them to believe that the other players were receiving electric shocks when they lost. When subjects believed they differed from the player in personality and values, they were less likely to intervene and help at their own expense (Krebs 1975). Recent neuroscience research traced this tendency to neural activity in the anterior cingulate cortex and showed that, at least in the case of race, we may be wired by default to respond less to the pain of people we perceive as different (Xu et al. 2009). These barriers to compassion inevitably take their toll, eroding the foundation to all kinds of prosocial, helping behaviors vital to the well-being of both individuals and societies alike (Eisenberg and Miller 1987; Helliwell and Putnam 2004).

A healthy sense of self is undeniably essential to our happiness, but when we feed the ego with an exclusive preference, and prop it up by pitting it against others, we extract a heavy price. When we fashion our sense of self in opposition to differences with others, whether real or imagined, we're creating gated communities in our hearts. We become implicitly attached to everyone on our side of the fence, while everything and everyone outside the gates looks more and more like a threat. This is the true danger in the self-centered tendencies of *asmita* that Krishna and Patanjali have been warning about. We're only okay inside as long as everything outside doesn't get too close. With that mentality, as Krishna said to Arjuna, how can we be happy here or anywhere?

Hope for the Helping Spirit

Now we are in a bind: the self we build to keep safe becomes a cage. The desire to cling to a stable and sheltered "me" amplifies the fear that adversaries are always waiting beyond the walls. At this point in the Gita, Krishna's command to Arjuna here is both illuminating and challenging:

> *The practice of yoga creates an equanimity of awareness,*
>
> *Seeing the Self in every being, and every being in the Self...*
>
> *The highest aim of yoga is to see all beings as equal,*
>
> *Whether in joy or suffering.* (6.29, 32)

Krishna suggests we need to open the gates and expand the walls. You are not the secluded little self you have imagined. And when you see your true Self, you will see how inextricably intertwined you are with every other being in the universe. The yoga tradition is stocked full of practices designed to deliberately blur the borders between us and our neighbors, emphasizing our interdependence rather than our independence. In some traditions of yoga and Buddhism, monks and renunciates are forbidden from eating anything that is not freely offered to them. Even though they have chosen to more or less retire from the outside world, every meal reinforces their dependence on the surrounding community. *Seva*—the concept of selfless service from the beginning of this chapter—keeps us at home in this world by constantly connecting us to our neighbors, holding the gates open for compassion. And, most important for us, meditation practice offers a deep toolbox for cultivating kindness and connection.

Metta Meditation

In the chapter on change, we began the practice of cultivating loving-kindness, or *metta*, with a focus on ourselves. Here, we'll expand that focus to a loved one, a neutral person, a challenging person, and, finally, all beings. However, like all the tools and techniques in this book, you should feel confident in adapting it in the ways that work for you.

Some meditators find it hard to start with themselves. Sharon Salzberg, a pioneer of *metta* meditation in America, often recounts a memorable story in which she asked the Dalai Lama whether it was advisable to start *metta* practice with oneself because she and so many of her students were frequently afflicted with feelings of self-hatred. The Dalai Lama seemed totally baffled that such an emotion even existed; he admitted that the Tibetan language had no such word for it. Yet when he asked the assembled Westerners whether they too ever felt such a thing, every single one raised their hand. Frankly, if you could take a listen in my head, you'd hear me say things to myself from time to time that I wouldn't say to my worst enemy. So if you've been struggling with the meditation on self-compassion since chapter 4, try starting with a loved one and working from there.

At Stanford's Center for Compassion and Altruism Research and Education (CCARE), a team led by Thupten Jinpa created a program based on *metta* meditation called Compassion Cultivation Training (CCT), and the CCT protocol starts compassion practice with a loved one precisely because so many people struggle with offering it to themselves (Singer and Bolz 2013).

You might prefer to start with a general focus on compassion for all beings and then work your way backward toward specific people. You might stay with just one individual for quite some time—days or even months. And you may choose to leave out a certain category if it's too challenging right now. It's not at all uncommon to come to a sticking point when you endeavor to bring compassion to a challenging or hurtful person. That's okay—offer what you can, where you can, and let that be enough. And, of course, if we can't think of an enemy, or anyone associated with negative emotions, the last thing we need to do is to try and dig one up or go inventing problems for ourselves. Start planting seeds wherever the soil is fertile for you, and see what sprouts up.

Inquiry: Spreading the Love

Give yourself twenty minutes in a place free of distractions. It may help to set a timer; if you have one that can sound at regular intervals, set it to chime once every three minutes. Settle into a comfortable position for meditation—alert but supported and at ease.

Begin by settling your focus on your breath, just as you've been practicing. Observe the inhale and exhale ebbing and flowing, feeling their movement within your body. When you notice the mind wandering, bring it back with a gentle, friendly attitude.

After a few minutes, when your timer chimes or whenever you are ready to transition, continue by returning to the meditation on self-compassion you cultivated in chapter 4. Holding in your mind's eye an image of yourself exactly as you are in this moment, offer yourself the following traditional mantra or a similar one that you create in the same spirit:

- *May you be happy.*

- *May you be healthy.*

- *May you be free from suffering.*

- *May you be at peace.*

As you breath in, say a single line of the mantra to yourself. Imagine the energy and intent of those words entering in with your breath and spreading into all corners of your body. As you exhale, let the breath go effortlessly and imagine it carrying away anything that's not needed right now. There's no need to pretend or try too hard. Simply feel what is actually present, and direct it with your breath and attention. Then move on to the next line of the mantra, and the next, and the next with each passing breath. If you experience any resistance, that's okay. And if other emotions arise, notice them. Come back to the mantra whenever you can. If obstacles become very strong, consider shifting your focus and offering the *metta* mantra directly to the obstacle itself. Continue in this way until the chime, or until you're ready to transition.

Now call into your mind's eye a loved one, perhaps someone who has shown great kindness and compassion to you in your own life or someone for whom you instinctively feel an impulse to express this mantra. Holding him or her in your awareness, offer the same wishes you offered to yourself. Again, imagine any energy or emotion evoked by these words circulating through you with the breath.

When it's time to continue, now call into your mind a neutral person, one of hundreds or thousands you may pass every day. There's no need to dig—take the first one that comes to mind and offer up the same good wishes you just offered to yourself and a loved one. Breathing in and out, line by line, continue to expand and direct your experience of loving-kindness.

When it's time to continue, call into your mind a challenging person, maybe someone who has hurt your feelings, or someone with whom there has been struggle. Maybe even someone you hate. As best you can, hold this person in your awareness and offer the same good wish, breath by breath. Offer what you can, where you can, and let that be enough.

Finally, let your awareness expand to embrace all beings, as if your mind's eye could become impossibly huge enough to hold those near and far, here and gone. As best you can, offer up the same mantra of loving-kindness to this vast sea of life, which includes you and everyone else you just held in your mind.

Now, release your focus from the *metta* meditation and return to your breath. Allow the inhale and exhale to take care of themselves while you simply watch. Notice any sensations or emotions that are present, and let them be just as they are. Notice what the meditation has left behind in you today, as well as anything else that has changed. When you are ready, open your eyes and mindfully return to your day.

The Consequences of Compassion

Metta meditation has been extensively studied, and its transformative potential ranks it the most promising single practice of any we've explored. If you seriously practice only one exercise from this entire book, I'd put all my money on this one. A study at Stanford's CCARE program on *metta* found that its CCT program successfully improved not only the ability to experience self-compassion but also the ability to express it and receive it from others (Jazaieri et al. 2013). FMRI studies led by Richard Davidson highlight how *metta* practices ignite neural structures associated with compassion, such as the insula and cingulate cortices of the limbic system (Lutz et al. 2008).

Inner compassion cultivated through *metta* can actually alter our behavior in the world outside. Remember the dictator game? People who practice *metta* meditation give significantly more of their money to their anonymous partner on the losing side (Reb, Junjie, and Narayanan 2010). In a variant of the game whereby subjects act as observers and can spend their own money to redistribute the wealth when they see the dictator screw the other partner over, compassion meditators give up substantially more of their own money in order to even the playing field (McCall et al. 2014; Weng et al. 2013). Compassion, it seems, converts the scrooge in all of us.

Those good wishes for all beings come right back around and hit us where it counts the most. Sustained *metta* meditation has been shown to decrease stress levels while increasing immune function; it's also shown to reduce pain and anger (Pace et al. 2009; Carson et al. 2005). *Metta* meditation may even slow aging: several studies have shown that frequent compassion meditators have longer telomeres—the caps on each strand of DNA that shorten as cells divide, leading the cell to eventually stop growing and ultimately die (Jacobs et al. 2011; Hoge et al. 2013). Shorter telomeres typically correlate with accelerated aging and deteriorating health. In some cases, meditation may not just slow that process but actually replenish the length of telomeres, allowing cells to survive longer (Schutte and Malouff 2014).

The role of telomeres in human health is still not completely understood, and while compassion may not be a fountain of youth, it will certainly help us enjoy the time we have. Positive psychologist Barbara Fredrickson found that a seven-week course in *metta* significantly increased participants' daily experience of positive emotions and their sense of social integration (2008). That feeling of social integration—of belonging and being connected in a community—may be the most crucial benefit of all.

The Ties That Bind Us

We are currently wading neck deep through a crisis of connection. Loneliness has been an accelerating epidemic in America for decades. In his landmark 1995 study "Bowling Alone," Robert Putnam chronicled three decades of free-falling civic engagement, marking the plummeting influence of social connectors of every kind, from union memberships to PTA meetings to the Boy Scouts, the League of Women Voters, the Masons, neighborhood card games, and just about everything in between. Putnam's conclusion is blunt and stark: "strands of social connection [are] being abraded—even destroyed—by technological and economic and social change" (1995, 382). Decades have passed since Putnam's work, and the tide is rising, not ebbing. Using results from the 2004 General Social Survey, the nation's most massive database of sociological information, researchers from Duke and the University of Arizona found that the average American reports only two close others to confide in. Twenty-five percent report no one close to them—a figure that jumps to half when family are excluded (McPherson, Smith-Lovin, and Brashears 2006). In the years since, social media platforms like Facebook and Twitter have proliferated, promising ever more connection, yet delivering greater and greater disconnect. A study by Robert Kraut in the late nineties tracked people during their first years of exposure to the Internet; he revealed that they became lonelier and more depressed the more they surfed the web (Kraut et al. 1998). While anybody who's anybody seems to be on Facebook these days, it also seems to be making everybody less happy: researchers at the University of Michigan found that the more often people used

Facebook, the less happy they felt in the moment and the less satisfied they felt about their life (Kross et al. 2013). It may be easier than ever to keep tabs on your old high school pals, but studies like these suggest that from across the vast distances of cyberspace we're not waving but drowning.

The cost of isolation in terms of well-being is incalculable. In his seminal 1943 work, "A Theory of Human Motivation," psychologist Abraham Maslow suggested that beyond basic needs like physical sustenance and safety, our primary human drive is one of connection—to know and be known by others, to give and receive care and love. Decades of subsequent research affirmed and amplified Maslow's hypothesis. A lack of social connection has been linked to increased mortality, even when controlling for general health and other risk behaviors (Berkman and Syme 1979). Later analysis of nearly 150 studies comprising more than 300,000 people concluded that social integration affects mortality as much as smoking or alcoholism—and that obesity and lack of exercise actually matter *less* (Holt-Lunstad, Smith, and Layton 2010). Loneliness literally hurts. When we feel alone and disconnected, it sparks brain activity in the anterior cingulate cortex—exactly the same spot ignited by physical pain (Eisenberger, Lieberman, and Williams 2003). Keep in mind, periods of distance and disconnect are inevitable. Psychologists have a term for people who sometimes feel lonely: totally normal. But when that feeling takes root and becomes the daily routine, danger arises.

Without exaggeration, your connection to others is the single greatest aspect of happiness that you can influence. In a study conveniently titled "Very Happy People," positive psychology pioneers Ed Diener and Martin Seligman screened more than two hundred individuals in an endeavor to shake out the common denominator in the happiest 10 percent. They found that no one variable was sufficient for happiness, but one proved absolutely necessary: good social relationships (2002).

Before you rush to reassure yourself by checking how many hundreds of contacts you have in your phone, keep in mind that quality, not quantity, measures social connection. Some of us need to cast a wide net and thrive best among many diverse companions, while some need just a couple close confidants. Whatever shape your social network takes, practices like *metta* meditation can deepen those ties tremendously.

Reconnecting

In this chapter, we've seen how distance and disconnect threaten our capacity for compassion. Given the epidemic of isolation just described, you might be expecting an uphill battle to bridge the gap. But the fruit of compassion may be surprisingly reachable. Remember that compassion thrives when we see someone as "like us"—and we saw earlier in Tajfel's experiments that what it takes for us to consider someone to be in our group can be almost arbitrary or incidental. Something as simple as moving in the same rhythms as another person—even just tapping a finger—has been shown to elicit both greater feelings of compassion and more altruistic behavior (Valdesolo and DeSteno 2011).

Metta meditation has been shown to increase feelings of social integration after even a *single* seven-minute session (Hutcherson, Seppala, and Gross 2008). If you've made it this far into the book, you've got seven minutes for meditation. And if you think you've got more time than that, the results are even more promising. Research on lifelong *metta* meditators by Richard Davidson used an electroencephalograph (EEG) to measure electrical activity in the brain during meditations on compassion. He found concentrated, coordinated waves of activity firing in a way that eclipsed anything ever seen in prior research (Lutz et al. 2004). Later fMRI research by the same team found enduring changes in neural structures associated with compassion for those who dedicated themselves to daily practice (Lutz et al. 2008). Remember: neurons that fire together, wire together. Research like this suggests that with even a bit of daily discipline, we too might become hardwired for compassion.

Take It to the Streets

All that compassion will do you, and everyone else, precious little good if it stays cooped up inside your head. If we take the Gita's challenge to heart, we need to put it into action. Just like we've done in meditation, we can start that practice with small seeds and grow from there. Sonja Lyubomirsky studied what happened when she challenged her students to perform five random acts of kindness in a week (Lyubomirsky, Tkach, and Sheldon 2004). Her results were somewhat unexpected: students who divvied up their kindness throughout the week emerged no different than the group that did nothing at all. But students who loaded up all their kindnesses into a single day were significantly happier *and* behaved in kinder ways throughout the week, even when they hadn't penciled extra kindness into their calendars.

This seeming paradox unravels a bit when we remember that, since kindness passes through the pleasure centers of the brain, it is subject to the same process of hedonic adaptation as all the other pleasures. Lyubomirsky hypothesized that students who diluted their kindness throughout the week weren't able to engage the circuitry of pleasurable giving beyond the threshold of an average day. But those who packed a day with several events sparked those synapses anew, and the effects of a single day of extraordinary kindness spread out into the following days. There may be a critical threshold for stimulating the pleasurable effects of kindness and making it more self-sustaining, but studies like Lyubomirsky's suggest it doesn't take a lot to trip that trigger. Once we've done that, compassion seems to move through our lives with an energy of its own.

INQUIRY: RANDOM ACTS OF KINDNESS

Tomorrow, commit to five extraordinary acts of kindness. An extraordinary act of kindness does not have to be hard to accomplish or represent a huge sacrifice on your part—it simply means that the acts you choose are beyond the normal activities you typically engage in every day. The kindnesses you choose could be almost anything at all: buying a cup of coffee for the person behind you in line at the café, holding a door for someone carrying a heavy package, giving up your seat on the subway, or bringing treats for coworkers. Some of them may arise spontaneously when you see someone in need or when a generous impulse strikes you, and others may be planned. Try to allow the day to unfold organically, without worrying about when or where your kindnesses will materialize. One of my students said that during this exercise she imagined the universe was conspiring to send opportunities for kindness her way, and all she had to do was keep an eye open. Keep yours open too.

Beyond self, Beyond Suffering

When we followed Patanjali's instructions to journey inward, we found that the ego we've been toting around is not so separate, and we began to unpack its heavy baggage, inquiring into what's left when so many stories and labels fall away. Patanjali invites us to seek the Self by making the self smaller and smaller through introspection. Now, Krishna guides us toward the Self through service and kindness, by making the self bigger and bigger. Who am "I" when I realize my self is so much the same as a friend, a stranger, or even an enemy? Who am "I" when the circle of the self begins to dilate and dissolve? We make these inquiries intuitively as relationships ebb and flow through a lifetime, and we build our rituals instinctively around the moments when our social selves undergo sudden change: a birth, a marriage, a death. Rather than waiting for the cradle or the altar or the gravestone to arrive, Krishna dares us to discover the Self by deliberately exploding the edges of our selves at every opportunity.

Some psychologists doubt how much room for renovation the self may hold, including leading altruism researcher Daniel Batson (from the famous Good Samaritan experiment), who writes that concepts such as "self-other merging…are best taken metaphorically rather than literally, at least when applied to empathy. The human capacity for empathy has a very wide range… [But] merging with and seeing oneself as psychologically indistinguishable from a convicted murderer seems unlikely; expanding the self to include a whale seems even less likely" (1997, 508). For Batson, altruistic behavior represents a "crossing the border" of oneself into the sphere of another, but the borders themselves remain unchanged. Yet other researchers in the same field have suggested that it's precisely this kind of self-expansion that stimulates much of our altruism. Psychologist Robert Cialdini posits that we're not in fact crossing the border but erasing it, at least momentarily. He found in his research that "When the distinction between self and other is undermined, the traditional dichotomy between selfishness and selflessness loses its meaning" (Cialdini et al. 1997, 490–91).

At the center of this rather academic debate lies the practical fact that, after thousands of years of divination, introspection, and experimentation, we still have remarkably little idea of what the self actually is, or how it comes into being, or exactly how it evolves through experience. In all its forms, the practice of yoga encourages us to experiment for ourselves with our selves. Whatever the self may ultimately be, whatever its limits and potential, in this chapter we've seen that so much of our happiness lies just beyond its familiar borders, intertwined in the lives of others. When we serve others and connect with compassion, that act transforms us physiologically, emotionally, and spiritually. Poet John Donne was right: no man is an island. If we imagine otherwise, we're sunk.

CHAPTER 8

Forgiveness and Gratitude: Look Back

The first recipe for happiness is: avoid too lengthy meditation on the past.

—André Maurois, author

Everyone loves a good revenge story—our fairy tales are full of them. And whatever revenges the fairy tales may have missed, soap operas have more than made up for. Revenge caters to our hope that injustices, big or small, cannot endure forever. It flatters our fantasies that we might restore the balance of the universe and personally deliver the punishments for those who've scarred our past. Try a taste of this tale of vengeance to whet your appetite:

Once upon a time, Olga married King Igor, and together they ruled over a vast empire. One day, Igor traveled to the neighboring country of Drevlian to collect a tribute from the people, who expressed their admiration by murdering him and throwing his body into a ditch. Afterward, the Drevlians couldn't help but notice that Queen Olga now sat on the throne all alone. So they sent over twenty of their best men to suggest that she marry the Drevlian prince, Mal. Olga politely demurred and buried the Drevlian ambassadors alive instead. Then she promptly sent word to Prince Mal that she would absolutely love to marry him, but she'd need a much larger group of his *very* best men to escort her to his castle for the wedding. So Mal sent an even bigger group to Olga, and when they arrived after a long and arduous journey, she welcomed them to unwind in her bathhouse. Then she locked the doors and burned it to the ground with all the men inside.

With all their best and very best men turning up missing every time they paid a visit to Olga, you'd think the Drevlians would start to smell a trap by now. Apparently not, because Olga next invited five thousand Drevlians to attend her husband's funeral, and they all showed up to pay their respects to the king they'd recently murdered. Once she got them all good and drunk with toasts, she had her soldiers slaughter the entire group. Figuring the Drevlians probably wouldn't be too keen on coming over for parties at her place anymore, Olga decided to pay them a visit herself— and then laid siege to their city.

With most of their soldiers long gone, the Drevlians surrendered and begged for mercy. Olga said she'd be glad to call it even if each Drevlian citizen gave her a gift of three doves—a small price to pay when the alternative is being run through with a spear. The Drevlians handed over their birds and probably would have been very happy to just leave Olga alone from then on, except that instead of heading home, Olga gathered all the doves and tied hot coals to their feet with strings, then released them. Like any sensible bird, the doves flew home, nestling into coops full of hay, and under the thatched roofs, and into nests across the city. Thousands upon thousands of cooing time bombs. Every building across the city burst into flame almost simultaneously, and Olga's army massacred the fleeing Drevlians, enslaving the few survivors. Then she lived happily ever after.

If you're wondering how you possibly missed reading a fairy tale as fantastic as the story of Queen Olga, it's because you were looking in the wrong place. She's in the history books, not the storybooks: Olga of Kiev ruled the Rus empire in what is now Eastern Europe from 945 to 963. Sometimes truth is stranger than fiction. But the happily ever after bit might have been a stretch on my part: she spent most of her remaining time warring with other kingdoms and dodging marriage proposals until she died of sickness while her own city was under siege. Since Olga had already seen how big funeral celebrations could go wrong, she requested to be buried alone with no ceremony. Later, she was named a saint by the Russian Orthodox Church (which was apparently willing to overlook some rather unsaintly behavior in her case).

Battling with Days Gone By

This chapter is all about our relationship to the past and how it shapes our happiness in the here and now. All of us have to grapple with the scars of our past; some of us on darker days have probably uttered a few prayers that would have been right up St. Olga's alley. How can we hope to dwell fully in the present moment when history has such a hold on us? Yoga points out a pathway to happiness that relies on the practice of being present, yet memory possesses a grip at least as strong.

In the Gita, when Arjuna comes to the battlefield and sees his *karma* staring back at him and armed to the teeth, we could scarcely blame him if he shows up thirsty for vengeance. The betrayals and deceptions of his cousins have cost him his homeland and thrust his family into years of exile. If my cousins stole my house and all my stuff and tried to kidnap my wife, I'd be plenty ticked off too. Yet again and again, Krishna counsels Arjuna toward equanimity even as he spurs him toward the fight. The contentment Krishna counsels comes not by imagining ourselves above the fray but by experiencing ourselves right in its midst. The point is not to settle the score but to do what is right for the world.

Desire and anger are voracious and dangerous.

Know that they are your true enemies. (3.37)

Let It All Out?

What, then, are we to do with all that pent-up aggression when we've been wronged? Isn't it bad to keep it bottled up inside? The idea that emotions gather inside us and need to be vented or expressed lest they fester and explode goes all the way back to the Greeks, if not farther. In Greek tragedies, dramatic tension builds to a moment of *catharsis*—literally "purging"—which releases the emotions of the audience and leaves them purified, usually by witnessing a moment of particularly grisly violence. Catharsis reads like a chorus line of Greek drama's most macabre moments: Oedipus pokes his eyes out, Medea kills her kids, and Clytemnestra hacks up her husband. Not exactly your typical feel-good matinee fare, but the

Greeks believed so much in the benefit of catharsis that nearly every tragedy stuck to the formula.

The cathartic theory of aggression works around the same idea—all that aggression has to *go* somewhere, or you'll be in trouble. To this day, most people think aggression works according to the cathartic model (Brown 1983). In recent decades, that belief led to much punching and screaming at pillows, pouring out our aggression on our home decor so it didn't end up spilling onto our loved ones. This is a great trend if you're in the business of selling pillows. There's just one problem: it's actually horrible for happiness.

Psychologist Brad Bushman teamed up with Roy Baumeister to tackle this topic head on. We last met Roy Baumeister in chapter 4 making people eat radishes and giving them impossible puzzles to solve, so you should be expecting some interesting experiments from these two. Together, they found that people who believe in the cathartic theory of aggression are much more likely to do things like hit a punching bag in order to make themselves feel better (Bushman, Baumeister, and Stack 1999; Bushman, Baumeister, and Phillips 2001).

Bushman later devised an experiment inviting people to write a brief essay on a topic, then hand it over to a (fictitious) partner in another room for "feedback," which always came back negative and full of insults. Some subjects were then invited to hit a punching bag, while others just waited a few minutes until the next part of the experiment. In the final stage, the subject and his or her "partner" played a game that tested reaction times by repeatedly pressing a button. After each press, the loser was hit with a blast of loud noise, ranging from 60 decibels (normal conversation) to 105 decibels (imagine laying your ear on a lawnmower). But here's the catch: in each instance, the winner determined the loudness and duration of the noise in the loser's ears. Again and again, the people who'd supposedly taken out their anger on the punching bag blasted their offending partners with louder and longer noises than those who just sat and stewed for a few minutes of "time-out" after being insulted (Bushman 2002). Turns out catharsis makes us more aggressive, not less. Now go apologize to your pillow.

The Price of Getting Even

But what if we end up happier, even with all the extra aggression? Sure, Olga of Kiev killed a lot of people to avenge her husband, but maybe after barbecuing all her enemies, she finally felt great. Research on more everyday revenges suggests not. After we punish someone, we tend to ruminate on the original harm and walk away angrier and unhappier than those who try to forgive and move on. Even worse, people consistently underestimate how unhappy they'll be after delivering punishment to their offenders or even witnessing someone else do it (Carlsmith, Wilson, and Gilbert 2008). If punishment so rarely helps us feel better for the little things like insults, it's probably not helping with regicide either. We need to take a closer look at what's going on here.

Psychologist Charlotte vanOyen Witvliet asked people to recall an episode when someone had truly hurt them in the past. She watched as their heart rate and blood pressure spiked, their faces tensed, and sweat began to pour—all hallmarks of the classic stress response. In Witvliet's experiment, as people recycled the memory of harm, their body relived the stress. And the body kept going well after the mind had moved on (Witvliet, Ludwig, and Vander Laan 2001). Just stewing with all that anger and angst wreaks havoc on the body, and subsequent research has tied regrets and grudges to increased depression and anxiety, and a general decline in well-being (Wrosch, Bauer, and Scheier 2005; Worsch et al. 2007; Roese and Olson 2014). Periodic anger is inevitable; it may serve as a healthy motivator to spur different behaviors moving forward. But at its worst it becomes a vortex that pulls us back again and again into the same current of negative, ruminating thoughts.

When we come to the battlefield swinging the hammer of vengeance, very often we end up hitting ourselves right in the face. In the language of yoga philosophy, extracting revenge and punishment create negative *samskaras*, carving deeper patterns of aggression, while failing to deliver on their promise of relieving unhappiness. No matter what triggers an emotion, whether someone cut you off on the highway or stole your family's whole kingdom, if we allow anger and hatred to repeatedly carve their way through consciousness, at the end of the day they're your burden to carry.

This is where the Bhagavad Gita's concept of justice becomes challenging and nuanced. Arjuna isn't instructed to just sit by and let his cousins take over the kingdom—Krishna commands him to fight for justice. But then Krishna reminds him again and again that if he heads into the battle looking for personal revenge, he's lost the war before the first arrow flies. He's been called to battle for the good of the kingdom; for Arjuna's *own* good, though, the harder road of contentment is prescribed.

Forgiveness

Witvliet's study also found an everyday antidote to the scars of anger: forgiveness. Participants who were asked to actively practice empathizing with and forgiving the person who harmed them showed a stress response much lower than those who let memory wash over them unchecked (2001). Forgiveness may be among the oldest and most common counsels of the world's great philosophies and religions; if anything, science is currently playing catch-up to millennia of wisdom encouraging us to forgive. Recent research has shown just how deeply transformative the practice of forgiveness can be. In multiple studies, people with a high aptitude for forgiveness showed lower blood pressure and lower resting cortisol levels, as well as better sleep, less fatigue, and fewer bodily complaints (Toussaint and Williams 2003; Lawler et al. 2005). In a survey of 1,500 people, those who actively practiced forgiveness reported greater life satisfaction as well as less nervousness, sadness, and restlessness. Moreover, the benefits of forgiveness compounded with age, suggesting that it is truly never too late to learn to forgive (Toussaint et al. 2001).

Stepping foot into the territory of forgiveness asks us to touch upon some of our deepest tragedies and traumas, and we should not trace those scars carelessly. As with revenge and aggression, misconceptions about forgiveness abound. One of the biggest obstacles to forgiveness can be the belief that, in forgiving, we're excusing bad behavior and letting injustice off the hook. In *Forgive for Good*, Frederic Luskin, director of Stanford University's Forgiveness Project, distinguishes forgiveness from any need to pardon or condone a transgression, or reunite a relationship (2002). We can hold a forgiving heart while still seeking justice or cutting ties. In fact, thoughts of forgiveness engage separate brain areas than considerations of fairness, with forgiveness pinging emotional centers in the limbic system and fairness focused in the cortex (Farrow et al. 2001). This may explain why finding forgiveness in the face of injustice feels so achingly impossible—when something feels unfair, it hijacks parts of the brain built for forgiveness. If anything, that suggests that the presence of justice frees us to forgive more easily. And that freedom goes to the forgiver.

Michael McCullough, a leading psychologist in the field of forgiveness, emphasizes that "When someone forgives a person who has committed a transgression…it is the forgiver who changes" (McCullough, Pargament, and Thoresen 2001, 9). Change of this kind invariably takes time and a process that does not unfold linearly. Tragedies and traumas create deep *samskaras*; they carve grooves in the self that cannot be easily smoothed. Forgiveness may be one of the best tools we have for repairing our own ability to sit in the present moment with contentment, but it is a tool that takes time to transform us. Hold it patiently with all the discipline, surrender, and compassion that you can muster.

INQUIRY: FINDING FORGIVENESS

There are many models for the process of forgiveness, but a simple and well-tested model that dovetails well with the practices we have been cultivating throughout this book was developed by psychologist Everett Worthington. He describes a five-step process called REACH—which stands for **R**ecall, **E**mpathize, **A**ltruism, **C**ommitting, and **H**olding On (Worthington 2008). Give yourself some quiet time free from distraction to explore this method with someone for whom you would like to cultivate forgiveness in mind.

- *Recall*: Call to mind the episode that hurt you, observing the memory and the emotions it brings as best you can.

- *Empathize*: Try to imagine the event from the perspective of the person who wronged you.

- *Altruism*: Remember a time in which you were forgiven, and recognize that you are now passing on the same gift to another.

- *Committing*: Publicly let your loved ones know that you have made a choice to forgive this person, and, if it feels appropriate, let him or her know as well.

- *Holding On*: When you recall the hurt, reconnect to your choice to forgive and continue the process anew.

The tools of meditation you've been practicing throughout this book go hand in hand with the REACH model. Recall can be done as a kind of meditation, watching the waves of thought and feeling as they rise and fall. Recognize ways in which you are now distant from that moment but still connected to it. As you cultivate empathy and altruism, you may choose to include this person in your *metta* meditation from the previous chapter. Acknowledge what arises as you endeavor to hold this person in the same compassion you offer to yourself and others, and watch how that compassion evolves as you return to the *metta* meditation over time. Doing so can strengthen your commitment and your ability to hold to the practice of forgiveness.

Setting the Story Straight

For many of us, there are people from our past who may feel too charged or challenging for the process just described. Fortunately, when the door to forgiveness feels locked and barred, there may be another point of entry to the past that's just as promising. Psychologist James Pennebaker ran an experiment in which he asked participants to write about their most traumatic experiences of the past for fifteen minutes each day for three days. He gave the writers no explicit goal other than to write freely and explore their thoughts and emotions without stopping; no need to try and forgive or empathize or move on—just write. Pennebaker disclosed that "As far as they knew, the purpose of the project was to learn more about writing and psychology" (1999, 1,244).

The results revealed much more than a writing lesson at work. Initially, subjects reported being less happy—no big surprise for anyone asked to delve into their most unhappy memories on a daily basis—but within days they reported being as happy or happier than those who were assigned to write on random topics, and it kept getting better from there. The writers showed increased immune function, and they reported less pain and fewer visits to a physician during the next several months, long after their writing stopped. Similar findings have been replicated and reviewed in nearly 150 separate studies, and the general results have held across boundaries of age, gender, culture, class, and personality type (Smyth 1998; Frattaroli 2006).

What's happening here? Pennebaker believes that the process of writing inherently forces people to channel complex and chaotic thoughts and emotions into the form of a narrative. We've been examining the self's penchant for storytelling throughout this book, and while the process of creating a self-narrative comes with a lot of pitfalls and blind spots that can get us into trouble, it is also a vital process for emotional well-being.

Your self and your stories are inseparable. You take it for granted that when you're on a date and someone says, "So, tell me about yourself," you're not supposed to reply, "I am a collection of molecules composed mostly of water, proteins, and fats that were first assembled in 1980." They're looking to hear about where you're from, what you do for work and pleasure, and how it is that you ended up wearing nice clothes at this fancy restaurant. They want to hear your stories. And if you want a second date, you'll want to tell them. Psychologists Kenneth and Mary Gergen go so far as to suggest that "we use the story form to identify ourselves to others and to ourselves... we live by stories—both in the telling and the doing of self" (1988, 17–18).

We've also seen how, left to its own devices, the voice in your head is not necessarily the most accurate storyteller. It's a bit like the ticker at the bottom of a cable news show—prolific and constant but also highly repetitive, rather jumbled, and obsessively focused on the negative. Meditation can turn down the volume on the storyteller—even give us enough peace and quiet to perceive the present moment in more detail—but the intent isn't to silence the stories altogether. That would be impossible. If anything, the intent is to realize that there is a fundamental process of storytelling at work inside you, and it's shaping you constantly. Perhaps most important, you can play an active role in how the stories are told. Pennebaker's writing exercise is an example of one arena where we can take advantage of the ego's narrative proclivities in service of profound healing.

Re-Storying

In Pennebaker's studies, the use of language proved extremely important for this re-storying process. Talking about personal experiences remains the foundation of most modern psychotherapies, and telling stories remains the typical way of talking about personal experience. Writing may serve a similar purpose. Simply thinking about past traumas most often leads to more of the same—rumination and unhappiness, digging the same negative *samskaras* a bit deeper with each go-round. After all, if you could just think your way free of the past and into the present, you'd probably have done that already. Movement expression like dancing didn't replicate Pennebaker's findings, either (Pennebaker and Seagal 1999). The expression of language, as much as it contributes to the complications of the self, also transforms it in unique ways.

Continuous writing straddles the gulf between the jumbled stories we constantly cobble together inside and the orderly expression of the stories we send out into the world. It lets in just enough of the real chaos and holds enough of a boundary that we don't get overwhelmed. For this reason, Pennebaker's writing exercise is not generally recommended for people with cognitive disorders, which often disrupt the typical process of creating self-narrative. And it hasn't been as effective for people with severe depression or PTSD, in which touching on a traumatic event often overwhelms the nervous system and hijacks the re-storying process. But for the vast majority of us, pouring our past into the crucible of language seems to invite an alchemy of memory, raw emotion, analysis, and expression that can be remarkably healing. The self emerges with a different story, and our relationship to the past evolves in the process.

Pennebaker's writing exercise implicitly acknowledges that we are all stuck with the storytelling self. To borrow a line we've heard before from Krishna in the Gita, "your own nature will drive you to it." The goal of Pennebaker's writing exercise isn't to stop the stories but to actively intervene in their production. Rather than sitting hunched over memories like tea leaves and taking whatever floats up to the surface of our attention as prophecy, in writing we delve in and engage with the story. We deliberately dust off the skeletons that are so tempting to leave locked away in the closet and hunt for thoughts behind thoughts, feelings inside feelings. In doing so, we "re-story" the self's darkest narratives. Just as *metta* meditation consciously shapes our capacity for compassion, writing refashions some of the oldest stories that made us who we are.

INQUIRY: WRITING DOWN THE PAST

You can give James Pennebaker's writing exercise a try for yourself. Here are the exact instructions he offered to subjects in his original experiment:

> *"For the next 3 days, I would like for you to write about your very deepest thoughts and feelings about an extremely important emotional issue that has affected you and your life. In your writing, I'd like you to really let go and explore your very deepest emotions and thoughts. You might tie your topic to your relationships with others, including parents, lovers, friends, or relatives; to your past, your present, or your future; or to who you have been, who you would like to be, or who you are now. You may write about the same general issues or experiences on all days of writing or on different topics each day. All of your writing will be completely confidential. Don't worry about spelling, sentence structure, or grammar. The only rule is that once you begin writing, continue to do so until your time is up." (Pennebaker 1997, 162)*

Dethroning Memory

Does re-storying mean that we're just turning a blind eye to the past and fabricating our feelings, glossing over the truth of our memory with a good fable? Pennebaker anticipated this problem by noting that "Ironically, then, good narratives can be beneficial in making our complex experiences more simple and understandable but, at the same time, they distort our recollection of them" (Pennebaker and Seagal 1999, 1,251). Yet the irony Pennebaker points out rests on a supposition that recollection holds more "truth" or authenticity than the result of a re-storying process. Memory seems to arise so vividly and effortlessly that we tend to think of it as flawless video footage we can instantly replay at any time. At least one large survey suggests most people do in fact believe memory works exactly this way (Simons and Chabris 2011).

Frankly, if you're still reading this book and thinking that your memories are faithful reproductions of the truth, then I'm guessing you skipped several chapters. Memory is as much the product of storytelling as all the other structures of the self, and it's compounded by countless biases that skew and color the story in ways that don't reflect what really happened or how we really felt at the time. A belief in the sacrosanct accuracy of memory props up the illusion that the self is something stable and permanent—an illusion we've been working hard to dispel from the beginning of this book. Whether we look from the perspective of *karma* and *samskara* or the vantage of neural plasticity, we find a self in constant flux, tethered to the past by a memory that has been through more retouching and selective editing than a tabloid.

Even if the fidelity of memory isn't flawless, not just any story will suffice. You are hardwired with a pretty finely calibrated emotional bullshit detector, and if you merely paint over your past with a broad brush of positivity, it will likely wash right off. Our oldest stories knit quite a knot of memory and emotion, and a lifetime of retelling pulls it tighter each time. Like meditation, the task here is to meet memories right where they live and see them exactly as they are with all their chaotic convolutions. Being honest with the emotional content of memory yields a more fruitful restorying process.

Through linguistic analysis, Pennebaker found that the most healing narratives actually contained a moderate number of negative words—neither censoring the gravity of the recollection nor obsessing over its content (1997). Part of the power in the writing exercise also lies in the insistence that writing be nonstop, which curtails the ability to carefully craft a polished-up version of the past and holds space open for genuine emotion to emerge. Writing for several days relieves any need to manufacture a meaningful story in one sitting. It allows the re-storying process to unfold organically, as it inevitably does when our past meets the present through language. This is an exercise in which the playing field of consciousness tilts in your favor. As much as we've been picking on the limits of attention throughout this book, when it comes to making coherence out of chaos, that's where consciousness is a rock star. You don't have to *try* to make sense of the memory; just write and let the story run its course.

The Good Times

For the majority of us whose past isn't loaded with memories of burying our enemies alive and setting birds on fire, there are probably a lot of pleasant moments to look back on. How should we handle the good stuff? Interestingly, the writing process we've just been exploring doesn't appear to be so useful here. Positive psychologist Sonja Lyubomirsky studied what happened when subjects were assigned to write about joyful moments and peak experiences using techniques similar to the Pennebaker exercise and found that writing about positive experiences had by and large no benefit in terms of happiness (Lyubomirsky, Sousa, and Dickerhoof 2006). The same sense-making power of re-storying that blunted the edge of our worst memories also dulls the memory of the magic moments we cherish. Analysis accelerates the inevitable process of hedonic adaptation. This appears to be the case not only for writing but for talking about experiences as well, since they share the same narrative constraints.

You may recall an experience from your past so sublime, so meaningful or pleasurable, that you've hesitated to even speak about it to someone else, even someone very close to you. Recent research suggests there's wisdom in that impulse. Psychologist Timothy Wilson theorizes that our innate tendency to "ordinize," or make sense of our experiences, drives more of that adaptation process than any other factor, so much so that "by turning the extraordinary into the ordinary, people rob events of their emotional power" (Wilson, Gilbert, and Centerbar 2003, 211). Making a story of the precious memories may serve another purpose, like bonding with a loved one, but it also saps some sweetness in the process.

Conversely, in Lyubomirsky's experiment, merely thinking about peak experiences showed a small but significant benefit in terms of positive emotion and life satisfaction, as every daydreamer can attest (Lyubomirsky, Sousa, and Dickerhoof 2006). When we just let the record of memory spin freely on a treasured groove, we can draw on its pleasure. Like any favorite song, though, eventually you'll have heard enough. The real place to search the past for happiness may lie in the everyday moments that so often pass us by without even making it onto our greatest hits list.

Gratitude

Psychologists Michael McCullough and Robert Emmons together studied the emotion of gratitude for many years. One of their seminal studies invited participants to keep a weekly gratitude journal chronicling five things, big or small, for which they felt thankful over the course of ten weeks. Quite a pleasant departure from getting shocked or having anonymous researchers insult your essay writing, or enduring any of the other indignities that have paved so much of the happiness research we've encountered so far. After the study, people who kept a gratitude journal reported being more optimistic and as much as 25 percent happier than a control group that merely listed their weekly activities. They also exercised on average an hour and half more each week than another group that kept a journal of things that annoyed them (Emmons and McCullough 2003). That's a pretty sweet trade-off just for taking a few extra moments to recall that time you snagged a great parking spot or caught a gorgeous sunset. Importantly, the gratitude journal didn't ask people to expound upon or analyze their thankfulness, simply to acknowledge it and express it for a line or two. All that was needed was to pass a grateful moment through consciousness again rather than letting it recede into the past.

Inquiry: Count Some Blessings

For the next several weeks, try keeping a gratitude journal of your own. Here are the simple instructions Robert Emmons and Michael McCullough gave to participants in their first gratitude study:

> *There are many things in our lives, both large and small, that we might be grateful about. Think back over the past week and write down... up to five things in your life that you are grateful or thankful for.* (2003, 379)

Positive psychologist Sonja Lyubomirsky created a similar exercise and found that weekly writers felt significantly happier by the end of the exercise, but daily journalers did not, possibly because the daily expression of gratitude became mundane and participants adapted to its repetitive joys as we all do (Lyubomirsky, Sheldon, and Schkade 2005). Which means you should feel free to adapt this exercise in the ways that resonate with you, whatever the frequency of your gratitude and however you express it. One longtime student of mine shared that, at bedtime, she and her young son pick "flowers" and "weeds" from their day: three "flower" moments he's happy for and one "weed" that made him sad.

The Gifts of Gratitude

Robert Emmons believes that gratitude accomplishes two basic but essential things for our well-being: it affirms that goodness exists, and it recognizes that goodness comes from outside the self (2007). The periodic affirmation of goodness counteracts the mind's negativity bias—the hardwired tendency we all have to dwell on bad things. In a sense, asking people to keep a journal of hassles and annoyances is redundant—when something goes wrong, your mind will replay that little ditty all day long without any effort on your part. Like neuropsychologist Rick Hanson says, your brain is like Velcro for the bad stuff and Teflon for the good stuff. Expressing gratitude helps make the good stuff stick, and we need all the help we can get with that.

Gratitude also highlights sources of goodness outside the self. While we're all predisposed to pay extra attention when things go wrong, we also love to take extra credit when things go right, even when we don't really deserve it. This little quirk of consciousness is called the *self-serving bias*, and it pops up in big and small ways in just about everything we do. Made it to the airport on time? That's because you are responsible and planned ahead. Missed your flight? That's because traffic was hell and other drivers are morons. An analysis of 266 separate studies found that self-serving bias differs somewhat from one culture to another, but we've all got it; kids and the elderly seem to have it the worst (Mezulis et al. 2004). Quote that last bit of research at holiday dinners at your own risk.

Self-serving bias becomes strongest in situations where the self feels threatened (Campbell and Sedikides 1999). This makes gratitude a particularly powerful antidote to self-serving bias because it puts the self in its place in a nonthreatening way. To bring our exploration back from the lab to the field of yoga, we can see how the self-serving bias caters to the causes of suffering (*kleshas*) and pulls us away from the reality of life. We build up a feeling of being a separate and sustaining self (*asmita*), which then requires constant maintenance to avoid the truth of existence, which is that the self is not really so separate and not all that sustaining (*avidya*). So we pat ourselves on the back extra hard when things go well in our lives because it makes the self feel more real and more valid (*raga*). But when something goes wrong, we have to push away our role in it lest it threaten the self we're clinging to (*dvesa*). It takes a lot of work to drag around the delusion that the self is so separate and significant. Softening the grip on the self can be terrifying but also tremendously freeing.

It seems far-fetched to suggest that a moment of gratitude as simple as saying, "I am thankful that someone smiled at me today," can pierce that veil, but it can. Gratitude is a subtle but significant reminder that we are not the ones responsible for so much of our happiness, as we saw in the previous chapter. When we recognize, again and again, that the self can't take sole credit for all our joys, we make a dent in some of that psychic armor and allow the self to become something much more porous and much less permanent.

When we soften self-illusion with gratitude, we not only let more happiness in, we send more out. Research by Monica Bartlett and David DeSteno has shown that experiencing gratitude increases helping behavior even more than being in a happy mood (2006). As we saw in the last chapter, altruism and kindness compound our happiness and creates deeper connections to those around us. Recent research suggests that when we feel close to those around us, the self-serving bias subsides significantly (Sedikedes et al. 1998; Campbell et al. 2000). Which in turn opens us up to even more gratitude, and the cycle continues. A little gratitude can go a long way, especially when it becomes the first step toward unbarring the doors of the self and welcoming in the reality that so much of our well-being is inextricably wrapped up in people and moments that our selves did nothing special to deserve.

The Paradox of the Past

The past is not an illusion we can simply dispel. Both yogis and psychologists find traces and trails of our history that impact what we can experience right here and now. Too often the attempt to "be present," as Buddha and Patanjali and Krishna have all implored us, leads to backward attempts to banish where we've been as if we could simply ignore it away and trade up for mindfulness in the here and now. So we don't look into the past's darkest corners for fear that shining attention into them could endanger our happiness. Ironically, if we meet those past hurts in the present with challenging practices of mindfulness and forgiveness, they may transform in time to support happiness rather than threaten it. Likewise, we often let everyday joys flicker through the present moment and fade when we could call them back with a gratitude that amplifies one of the most potent sources of happiness we have: a compassionate connection to the people and the world around us. The paradox of our past is that only when we fully engage with it are we free to experience the present moment as it is. We learn to draw upon the past without dwelling in it. From there, we're free to plot a course for the future, which is where we're headed next.

CHAPTER 9

Goals:
Look Ahead

Chase after money and security
and your heart will never unclench.
Care about people's approval
and you will be their prisoner.
Do your work, then step back.
The only path to serenity.

—Lao-tzu, philosopher and poet

Right after Krishna tells Arjuna to get up off his butt and get into battle, he saddles the downtrodden warrior with the Gita's most perplexing dilemma:

You are entitled to action, but never to its results.

Let your action be an end unto itself, and do not cling to inaction. (2.48)

Krishna's call to action comes with a catch. From one corner of his mouth, he tells us to give it all we've got; from the other, we're told to let go of the outcome completely. Put your whole self in, and take your whole self out, all at the same time. If that kind of spiritual hokey-pokey has you stumbling over yourself, you're in good company: Arjuna finds this concept so mind-boggling that Krishna will end up explaining it to him nearly a dozen different ways during the course of their conversation.

The problem we share with Arjuna is that action is unavoidable and yet inextricably tangled up in stories of the self and the side effect of suffering. It seems like we're damned if we do, and damned if we don't. The Gita's greatest and most challenging promise is that there's a way to engage in action without getting hooked by suffering.

> *One who perseveres in yoga and surrenders the fruit of action finds perfect peace.*
>
> *But one who clings to the fruit is bound by desire in everything.*
> (5.12)

What could Krishna possibly mean by surrendering the fruit of action? He goes so far as to say that when we do, we're freed from the bonds of *karma* and *samskara.* So do we head into work tomorrow to let the boss know we'll be surrendering our salary, but we'd like to keep the job because we could really use the action? Perfect peace sounds great, but, at first glance, the cure for suffering looks worse than the disease. How do we plan a life or set goals when the future is littered with fruit ripe for surrender? This chapter explores the road from here—how we unlock the puzzle of action without attachment and chart a course for the days ahead.

The Ant and the Grasshopper

When I was a little kid, Aesop's fable "The Ant and the Grasshopper" drove me absolutely crazy. All summer long, the Grasshopper leaps through the fields, frolicking and chirping, while the Ant does nothing but toil away gathering food for the oncoming winter. The Grasshopper plays in the present moment while the Ant focuses on the future. When the frost sets in, the Grasshopper, shivering and starving, sees the Ant with plenty to eat and realizes the error of his ways too late. I've found many versions of the fable, but I can tell you from vivid memory that in the daycare where I first heard the story, it ended with the Grasshopper dead every time. The lady who ran that daycare apparently had a pretty macabre work ethic. I was probably supposed to learn the value of planning ahead, but the whole thing just seemed very tragic at the time. A care-free Grasshopper perishes like a popsicle, and a puritanical Ant who's never had a day of fun in his life sits atop a mountain of more food than he can eat. Even as a five-year-old the whole story sounded grossly unsatisfying.

Aesop and the Ant have some solid psychology on their sides. Edwin Locke, one of the leading psychologists studying goal setting, found that planning and creating goals leads to better performance, more sustained effort, and more focused attention (Locke and Latham 2002). We know that willpower and conscious attention are finite resources; having a goal channels that mental energy so that less is wasted along the way. When Krishna tells Arjuna that "yoga is skillfulness in action," he sounds like he ought to be a big fan of goals. So why all the surrender?

Making progress toward goals increases well-being, and progressing toward harder goals makes us happier than approaching finish lines that are easy to cross (Wiese and Freund 2005). This is why kids love the game Candyland and adults loathe it. For kids, learning colors and counting and taking turns is an elaborate and mystical ritual. To a grown-up, playing Candyland feels like being locked in a perverse and predestined sugar-coated hell. There's absolutely no skill or challenge to be had. Finding both meaning and flow require us to grapple with goal setting. No one would train for the Olympics if there were no medals to win or records to set. Wherever passion and purpose may point us, we're left to wander if we can't set goals. Stretching to the edges of our possibility and shaping our future is integral to well-being, and, at first glance, reaping the reward of hard-won goals looks like a good thing for happiness. Frolicking in the fields may be fun, but keeping eyes on the prize channels our potential in an entirely different way. Score one for the Ants.

But the prize itself makes a very big difference. Consider the Candle Problem, devised by psychologist Karl Duncker. If you snagged a spot in Karl Duncker's lab, you'd find yourself alone in a room with a table containing only a book of matches, a box of thumbtacks, and a small birthday candle. Your job is to light the candle and stick it to the wall in such a way that the wax won't drip onto the table below using only the items provided. You can take a minute to puzzle it out in your head, or dig around in your drawers to see if you have what you need to play the game on your own, but I'm about to spoil it if you don't stop reading right now. The solution, which most people miss for quite some time, is to empty out the box of tacks, tack the box to the wall and use it as a candle holder (Duncker and Lees 1945). The problem demonstrates the concept of *functional fixedness*—people see the box as a holder for tacks and typically miss that it can be used to hold a candle just as well.

The candle problem had nothing to do with goals and rewards until it got into the hands of Sam Glucksberg, a psychologist who wanted to see how much better people became at solving it when he gave them the incentive of winning money (1962). Some folks came into Glucksberg's experiment and tackled the puzzle just for the fun of it, while others were told that they'd get $20 if they solved it fastest, or $5 if they landed in the top quarter—not a bad day's work for problem solvers in 1962. How much did the goal of cold, hard cash increase people's performance? On average, it took them three and a half minutes longer to solve the candle problem. That's not a typo—the promise of a reward made them perform *worse*. A lot worse. Sometimes our goals for the future mess us up right here in the present moment. Score one for the Grasshoppers.

The Trouble with Goals

In the candle problem, the external incentive of money focused participants—but in the wrong place, diverting precious attention to the prospect of winning or losing money instead of engaging in creative problem solving. In puzzle experiments led by Edward Deci, participants who were paid to play ended up playing less once rewards were removed, whereas people who were paid nothing continued to tinker long after the clock had stopped (1971). Deci later teamed up with Richard Ryan to expand on this idea and demonstrate that the reward of money saps not only creative thinking but also motivation for sticking with complex and challenging tasks. They analyzed 128 separate studies on motivation spanning decades, all pointing to the same general principle: when we attach external rewards to an activity that should be intrinsically engaging, our motivation for doing what we do becomes bound up in the reward (Deci,

Koestner, and Ryan 1999). We get hooked on the fruit and lose interest in the action itself.

In one experiment, preschoolers at playtime were given two equally beloved activities, then told that they had to do one first in order to be able to do another. Want to finger paint? Five minutes of storytime first. You have to pet the kitty before you can go on the swings. In every instance, kids found the activity presented as a means less enjoyable than the activity chosen as the end (Lepper et al. 1982). The arrangement in the experiment was totally arbitrary—it didn't matter whether kitty came first and swings were second or the other way around—just positioning one fun activity as a reward made the other less fun. When we do what we do to get something else, we become less interested in whatever it is we're doing.

But external rewards have their place. As Daniel Pink puts it in his book *Drive*, which expounds on Deci and Ryan's body of research, carrots and sticks are superb motivators for chores we hate, tedious tasks, and all the boring stuff we love to put off (2009). They're great for tasks that harbor no intrinsic interest. If you spend all day at work scrubbing toilets or cranking out widgets in a factory assembly line, then attaching a reward to your performance is likely to improve it. In those activities, there's little to no intrinsic motivation to lose. But for complex, creative, challenging things, rewards interfere with our actions.

And what could be a more complex, creative, and challenging task than the pursuit of your own happiness? This journey demands intrinsic motivation more than any other—arguably, there is *nothing* more intrinsic than your happiness. If we start dangling too many external rewards out in front of the path, we just end up addicted to carrots. It's the story of every person who landed a job doing what they loved only to find that their new profession slowly drained their passion. We find more joy along the journey when, like the Grasshopper, we're able to be immersed in what we're doing for its own sake.

Don't Set Your Sights on Happiness

Paradoxically, this means that setting happiness up as the goal can become a self-defeating pursuit. When we bumped into Aristotle at the beginning of this book, he called happiness the whole aim and end of human existence. But with a pedestal so high, we risk placing happiness beyond our own reach.

Eleanor Roosevelt famously said, "Happiness is not a goal...it is a by-product of a life well lived." The former First Lady may have been onto something. Like being paid for puzzles or anything else we're intrinsically interested in, making a goal of happiness puts attention in the wrong place. In an experiment led by Jonathan Schooler, three groups of subjects all listened to Stravinsky's *Rite of Spring*. The first group tried to make themselves as happy as possible while listening, whereas the second monitored and reported their moment-to-moment joy on a computerized "happiness meter," and the control group let the music flow through and just listened. Both trying to maximize happiness and paying constant attention to it made people *less* happy. The happiest people didn't try to be happy or even think about whether they were. They just listened (Schooler, Ariely, and Loewenstein 2003).

Happiness is slippery like that. Trying to hold on to it often makes it spring a leak. Trying to inflate it drains it even faster. We can't experience happiness without conscious attention, yet attention can so easily undermine it. Because conscious attention can basically be just one place at one time, when we shift focus to whether we're happy or trying to pump up our positive emotions, we have to move attention away from the music—the very spring that started the feeling flowing in the first place.

Research on the relationship between mood and attention is complex and evolving. A growing body of research suggests that sad moods induce greater self-focused attention, and happier moods draw less attention toward oneself (Wood, Saltzberg, and Goldsamt 1990; Green et al. 2003). If this relationship is a two-way street, it's very possible that excessive self-directed focus can impede positive emotions like happiness. One of the largest analyses, spanning 226 separate studies, suggests precisely that (Mor and Winquist 2002). Nothing creates focus like having a goal—all your attentional resources line up to answer the call. But if the goal is your happiness, there's only one place for all that focus to go: right back onto you. And the very self-focus designed to monitor your progress toward happiness may short-circuit the whole process. We need to get out of our own way, get our mind back on the music, and let happiness arise as a side effect just as Mrs. Roosevelt described. Score one for the First Lady.

Let Your Action Be an End Unto Itself

The tensions between happiness and attention dovetail well with what we know about the experience of flow—the sense of deep and self-transcending engagement that arises in challenging and passion-driven activities. In moments of flow, ego evaporates as we become fully absorbed in the activity at hand, and people frequently report moments of flow among their very happiest. Though flow activities very often entail goals, people in flow typically describe the action as its own reward. Pioneering flow researcher Mihaly Csikszentmihalyi called these behaviors *autotelic*, from the Greek words for "self" and "goal." He theorized that people capable of great flow had autotelic personalities in that they "generally [do] things for their own sake rather than for some later external reward" (1990, 117). In autotelic actions, the goal serves as a steering device, like a compass to keep us on course rather than a destination we have to get to. In flow, the joy is in the journey. The effort is its own reward. I think Krishna's ears just perked up.

Subsequent research revealed that autotelic personalities boil down to a handful of common traits, "or competencies that enable the individual to enter flow and stay in it… [including] curiosity and interest in life, persistence, and low self-centeredness, which result in the ability to be motivated by intrinsic rewards" (Nakamura and Csikszentmihalyi 2002). Take a look at how snugly the three qualities he singles out—persistence, curiosity, and humility—fit with the pillars of yogic action that Patanjali laid out for us in the *Yoga Sutras*:

Yogic action requires discipline, self-study, and surrender. (2.1)

From very different approaches, yoga and psychology arrive on remarkably solid common ground. The foundational principles of yogic action and the key components of autotelic action are practically identical. We have to become eager to inquire into ourselves and our world. We need the grit and determination to hone and challenge the self we've been given. And, ultimately, we need to be willing to surrender that sense of self enough to become absorbed in what we do. When it comes to the kind of actions that make us happiest, psychology and yoga philosophy are in deep agreement here; and in the context of intrinsic and extrinsic goals, Krishna's command to surrender the fruit of our actions starts to make a lot more sense.

Inspiration from Within

In the pursuit of happiness, we're at our best when we go after goals that express something internal rather than attain something external. Experiments by Tim Kasser and Richard Ryan found that people whose principle goals were wealth, status, or image reported less well-being than those who built their lives around intrinsic goals of health, growth, relatedness, or kindness (1996). Not only do people with intrinsic goals bring greater effort to their pursuit, they are more likely to reach their goals (Sheldon and Elliot 1999). Along with his partner Edward Deci from the puzzle experiments, Ryan expanded this research over decades to form *self-determination theory*, which posits that the capacity for intrinsic motivation is innate to the human condition and driven by three basic and essential psychological needs:

> **Autonomy:** the need to feel like a coherent and integrated self, and to have a sense of agency in what that self does.
>
> **Competence:** the need to grow the self and shape its environment through mastering skills.
>
> **Relatedness:** the need to connect the self to others through caring and being cared for. (Deci and Ryan 2002)

We've been exploring these three needs through the lens of yoga throughout this book. At first glance, autonomy might raise an eyebrow, because it looks a lot like ego, or *asmita*, in disguise. The self can be a slippery slope to suffering, but the autonomy described by self-determination theory has much less to do with the stories of the self and much more in common with mindfulness:

When individuals function autonomously, they are open to the experience of what is occurring in the current moment… [They] have a higher tolerance for encountering experience without being threatened or defending against it… [They are] responsive to reality rather than directed by ego-invested preconceived notions. (Hodgins and Knee 2002, 88–89)

Krishna and Patanjali would both give a big thumbs up to that kind of self.

We've seen the quality of competence expressed in everything from Krishna's command to "transform your self with the Self," to his explanation of yoga as "skillfulness in action." For Patanjali, the whole project of self-transformation is anchored in discipline (*tapas*) and practice. Mastering the ability to shape the self skillfully and accept its limits humbly is the heart of the entire yoga mission.

Relatedness intersects with the practices of compassion and the meditations on loving-kindness central to the chapter on connection. Patanjali's inward path starts with the *yamas*—ethical principles for relating to those around us. He instructs us not to abandon the external world but to care for it in a way that frees us to inquire within and frees others to do the same. We untangled the whole story of the self by first pulling on the thread of separateness, and as the illusion of separateness unraveled, we glimpsed a Self intimately and inextricably related to others. And when Krishna coaxes us out into the world, he reminds us, "Without the spirit to serve…how could one be happy here or anywhere?"

Inquiry: Gauging Goals

Set aside some time to consider an important goal you have for the future. Are there things about this goal that are extrinsic—measured by someone or something outside yourself? Are there aspects of the goal that feel intrinsic, in that they express some trait or value that feels integral to who you are? Keep in mind that many goals are not purely extrinsic or intrinsic, and yours may have elements of both.

Where the goal feels intrinsic, how does it tap in to your drive for autonomy, competence, and relatedness? Are there signature strengths or other important traits that this goal calls upon or cultivates? Are there ways you'd like to adjust or hone this goal to emphasize those aspects? Sometimes becoming aware of the deepest roots of an intrinsic goal can help us avoid being lured astray by external rewards along the way.

Where the goal feels extrinsic, are there ways you can reframe it to include and encourage intrinsic motivation? Are there things you might do in pursuit of this goal that are flow activities for you? Keep in mind that extrinsic goals are not bad, and they are sometimes inevitable for all of us. Often, extrinsic goals can be stepping stones toward much larger, more intrinsic goals. Are there ways the extrinsic part of this goal serves broader or deeper intrinsic motivations in you?

Action without Attachment

When goals reflect the deepest intrinsic motivations of one's authentic self, we can act wholeheartedly without getting hooked on results. You can enjoy the fruit without getting attached to it. You don't have to give back your salary, or turn in your trophies, but you do need to remember why you came to the battlefield in the first place. All those rewards are symbols of hard-fought goals—and only symbols. The Gita isn't asking us to surrender caring about the causes that will better our world. If anything, it asks the opposite. Passion for a purpose imbues you with a dedication and drive that psychologists would say is quintessentially human, and I think Krishna would concur. That's why he tells Arjuna to fight. But when achieving that purpose defines you, suffering is sure to follow whether you triumph or not. That's why he tells Arjuna to let go. This is the paradox of goals: they look like tools to secure a better future, but they serve us best when they free us to engage more openly with the present moment.

CHAPTER 10

Look Again

I kept as still as I could. Nothing happened... I was entirely happy. Perhaps we feel like that when we die and become a part of something entire, whether it is sun and air, or goodness and knowledge... That is happiness; to be dissolved into something complete and great. When it comes to one, it comes as naturally as sleep.

—Willa Cather, novelist

Enduring happiness arises in the pursuit, and in the self it enables us to experience and express. The better we know the self, the more skillfully we can express it, which is why we spent the first half of this book spelunking in the caverns of consciousness. Ultimately, the Gita encourages our self-expression to take the form of service, which is why so much of the latter half has centered on finding purpose and connection. Happiness requires both self and selflessness to thrive. If your heart's not in it, you suffer; but if it's all about you, you suffer too. When we bring forth the deepest aspects of the self in service of something greater than ourselves, we are treading the trail of *dharma*, and our actions free us rather than bind us.

A Call to Worship

But Krishna has one more little thing to add. In the Gita's final chapter, he whispers to Arjuna that among all actions, three kinds have a special place in liberating us from the cycle of suffering.

Actions of self-discipline, service, and worship should never be abandoned,

For these purify and lead to wisdom.

Yet even these actions should be undertaken without attachment.

This is my highest belief. (18.5–6)

We've looked at self-discipline and service from a variety of angles, but what are we to make of worship? At the beginning of this book, I promised we wouldn't be grappling with God. But in the end, Krishna just won't let us avoid it. Again and again throughout the Gita, he instructs Arjuna to turn his wisdom into work and his work into worship, and to devote all his actions to divinity. Which in this case happens to be Krishna himself. Naturally, Arjuna has questions, and we should too.

How will I know you when I see you, and where should I direct my meditations?

What aspects of existence can I think on to find you, Krishna? (10.17)

If the Gita sets worship up on such a high pedestal, we'd all do well to know what's worth worshiping, and Krishna's reply is telling.

I am the Self resting within all beings;

From the moment they begin their being to their very end. (10.20)

But Krishna doesn't stop there. For the next twenty lines, he expounds on the infinite corners of existence where divinity may be encountered, from the stars to the moon, from the oceans to the mountains. He points to divinity in trees, in birds, in cows and lions and serpents. He finds divinity in the mind, in knowledge, in logic, in speech, and in silence. He finds something sacred in honest people speaking truth, then sees the same in cheating gamblers. He points to the poets, the sages, the generals, and to Arjuna himself. Finally, as the list grows full and overflows, Krishna concludes:

I am the seed of everything, Arjuna.

In the still and moving universe, there is nothing that exists but through me.

The manifestations of divinity have no end.

These are but an example. (10.39–40)

If we're worried that at the last minute the Gita denies the possibility of happiness unless we bow down to a bright blue Hindu avatar, we needn't be so literal. In the end, Krishna concludes, you can find a spark of divinity in anything if you know how to look. Anywhere can become a place to worship if you choose to do so. The choice to worship more than the object makes the difference. As poet Wallace Stevens wrote, "It is the belief and not the God that counts."

An Echo from Patanjali

When we explored change with Patanjali in the fourth chapter, he came down squarely on the side of faith as well. In addition to the discipline of *tapas*, and the self-study of *svadyaya*, Patanjali finally called for surrender, or *ishvara pranidhana*. And to make tough changes stick, that sense of devotion seems to be essential.

Whenever we work to change our lives or our world, moments of doubt are inevitable. Surrender in this context builds a scaffolding made of faith that sustains you until the discipline of your practice can set and cement new behaviors. Without faith to hold on to, doubts and distractions may be misinterpreted as signs that we're going the wrong way.

From Patanjali's yogic perspective, *ishvara pranidhana* keeps us on track when we've exhausted everything we've got, while *tapas* keeps doing our damnedest to dig in with every fiber of our being, and *svadyaya* helps us understand where the edges of our ability really are. If all that ancient Sanskrit sounds oddly familiar right now, it might be this little gem of a prayer sparkling in the back of your brain:

God, grant me the Serenity to accept the things I cannot change; the Courage to change the things I can; and the Wisdom to know the difference.

That's the Serenity Prayer, attributed to Reinhold Niebuhr in the 1930s and found in 12-step programs worldwide. You'll find the very same values tucked away inside Patanjali's little manual on how to change your mind, from nearly 2,000 years earlier. Great ideas tend to stick around.

Today, one of the most effective practical programs for creating lasting change in the face of strong resistance is Alcoholics Anonymous. In *The Power of Habit*, Charles Duhigg profiles the ways that AA's twelve steps for sobriety integrate the discipline of meetings and new routines with the self-study required to take rigorous account of one's triggers for drinking and the people they have wronged. Science has studied AA for some time and had a solid grip on how discipline and self-assessment were at work in the program. But researchers were stymied by the particular importance many members place on the third step—surrender—involving a "decision to turn our will and our lives over to the care of God as we understand Him," as the saying traditionally goes. Shouldn't discipline and self-awareness alone be sufficient? Clearly not:

> [A]lcoholics who believed... that some higher power had entered their lives were more likely to make it through stressful periods with their sobriety intact. It wasn't God that mattered, the researchers figured out. It was belief itself that made a difference... Belief was the ingredient that made a reworked habit loop into a permanent behavior. (2012, 84–85)

To Know One's Self

Whether you call it surrender, serenity, or worship, the shape it takes will be intimately unique to you. As the poet Rumi wrote, "There are hundreds of ways to kneel and kiss the ground." Rather than telling us what to pray to and how to do it, I think Krishna is pointing to the absolute necessity that we make the final, sober confession that the self is at sea in something so much larger and so much greater than we may ever comprehend. Whatever that may be—soul or Self or stillness or absolute emptiness—it is the essence of everything we are and everything we encounter. The Gita counsels us to devote ourselves to knowing that essence in spite of its utter unknowability. It's a battle worthy of a great warrior.

As the Gita unfolds, Arjuna learns of the Self and yearns to experience it, just as we may long for it in moments of meditation or prayer or contemplation. There on the battlefield, he asks Krishna for a favor: to show him the Self, to experience life as it really is, if only for a moment. Krishna's initial response is simply, "Look again, Arjuna." Just look. Look at the infinite colors and shapes and wonders of the universe. It's all right there, happening right now. But finally Krishna acquiesces to his friend, saying:

You are not able to see with mortal eyes,

so I will give you divine sight: now, look! (11.8)

What follows is one of the most dramatic scenes of revelation in all of world literature. Krishna pulls away the veil of the mind, and instead of being focused in one place at one time, Arjuna suddenly sees everywhere, all the time, all at once. Instead of the usual forty bits he knows through the narrow window of consciousness, instead of even the eleven million bits taken in by his senses, he experiences an infinite, instantaneous flow of information. Krishna becomes the creation and destruction of all time and existence, and Arjuna witnesses it all in a single moment. No longer a separate little drop, he is dissolved again into the vast and churning ocean. Unable to bear so much, he collapses, begging for his mortal vision and his familiar friend to return.

Krishna releases the vision and consoles Arjuna by telling him that the fullness of the Self is impossible to comprehend and something that mortals never completely experience. To be fair, he had warned the warrior only moments before:

But what would you do with so much knowledge, Arjuna?

Just know that a single sliver of my being supports the entire universe.
(10.42)

It's attractive to hold an idea of enlightenment that looks a lot like Arjuna's vision: *If I work hard enough, or believe the right things, or pray the right way, in a moment all will be revealed. Until then, whatever I'm experiencing, that's not enlightenment.* Notice how often we carry the same attitude toward happiness: *If only I can get this, then I will be happy. If only I can avoid this, then I will be happy. Until then, I can't be happy.* If that's our road map, bliss is always somewhere else.

But when Arjuna asks for instantaneous enlightenment, Krishna's reply is, "Just look." It's always already there. And when Arjuna's fervent wish for total and instant illumination is granted, it's too much to handle. He's like the dog that finally caught the car. We ought to consider that enlightenment may happen for us another way.

The Color of Clarity

There's a parable often attributed to Maharishi Mahesh Yogi, creator of Transcendental Meditation, which imagines enlightenment in the way that someone might slowly dye a cloth. You begin by soaking the cloth in a vat of color, leaving it there for some time. Then you hang it to dry in the sun. As the sun beats down, it weathers the cloth and strips much of the color away, yet some remains behind. Then you return it to the vat and soak it again, and hang it once more in the sun. Again the sun beats down, and again the color fades, but more lingers than before. And so on and so on, from soaking to sun and back, until gradually the color and the cloth become inseparable, and the fabric takes on a tone that time and circumstance cannot strip away.

When we tell the story of enlightenment this way, there is no final instant of illumination. After the first soaking, the color is bright but unstable and prone to fade at the slightest challenge from the sun. The sun, which seems like a hindrance, ultimately fixes the color and makes it enduring. In this view, the distractions and frictions of daily life are just as vital to the process as immersion in the insights within. Time and repetition are essential ingredients, as is a willingness to accept the inevitable fading along with the gradual deepening.

Both Krishna and Patanjali encourage us to take this longer road and learn how to handle the self and seek the Self by degrees, taking in what we can where we can with the understanding that bliss has no border we will finally cross over and call home. You can't really live there, but you never really leave there, either.

Krishna might go so far as to say that a life spent only soaking up color in the vat is a life wasted. Whatever Self you encounter within, whatever name you come to call it by, that Self is not yours. It does not belong to you. It belongs in the world. The reason *you* are there is to carry that spark of Self home, to dissolve it back into the universe as an offering. In the Gita, this is described as our highest duty. Legendary dancer and choreographer Martha Graham hit on this aspect of *dharma* so clearly that she might have taken the words right out of Krishna's mouth:

> *There is a vitality, a life force, an energy, a quickening that is translated through you into action, and because there is only one of you in all of time, this expression is unique. And if you block it, it will never exist through any other medium and it will be lost. The world will not have it. It is not your business to determine how good it is nor how valuable nor how it compares with other expressions. It is your business...to keep the channel open.* (quoted in De Mille 1991, 264)

Holding On and Letting Go

After I barfed away my future as an economist at the beginning of this book, I decided to just go ahead and do the foolish thing and pursue a life in the theater full-time. Within a couple years I was lucky to land a spot in Harvard's graduate theater program, studying the great stories of humanity, how to shape them and share them. When I wasn't busy on the stage, I was sneaking into Tal Ben-Shahar's packed positive psychology class across campus or wandering. I wandered into yoga to try and touch my toes. Little did I know at the time.

The more I studied yoga and psychology, the more I came into contact with my own stories, the more I understood how they shaped me, and the more I realized the potential to bend the arc of my own life. Today, as a teacher of yoga and its philosophy, fascination with the fictional stories of the stage has faded, and I've grown to love the real-life stories that play out in the bodies and minds of millions upon millions of people on the yoga mat and the meditation cushion around the world. You just can't beat real life. Beneath all these pursuits, I see the same basic questions that have driven this book and the questions I believe drive us all: "Who are we?" "What's real?" and "What should we do to be happy?"

Yoga and the Pursuit of Happiness began with three very different views of happiness from Aristotle (virtues in action), Aquinas (communion with divinity), and the Dalai Lama (compassionate connection to others). I wondered which we might look to for our own well-being.

We must act, to express our deepest strengths and to shape our own world with purpose and passion.

We require connection with something greater than ourselves, be it the mystery of God or the simplicity of stillness.

And ultimately we need one another; whatever secrets we may realize within or beyond, community is a certain key to happiness that could be sitting next to you right now.

We ought to pursue happiness in *all* these places. Doing so is our *dharma*, a call to action to our very core that cannot be ignored. We should seek it like our lives depend upon it. They do.

Now, this is the inquiry of Yoga…

Now, arise and fight…

Acknowledgments

Thanks to Wendy Millstine, who called me up out of the blue one day from New Harbinger and asked if I wanted to take ideas I'd been speaking on for a decade and turn them into a book, and then asked again until I had the sense to say yes. Thanks as well to the countless editors and commenters who took things I've been talking about for ten years and helped me put them on the page in a way that makes me sound way more eloquent than I am.

I have been lucky to have teachers too numerous and inspiring to properly thank, but two in particular shaped my journey as a yoga teacher so much that I could not write this book without offering special gratitude: my first mentor at Kripalu, Yoganand Michael Carroll, and my longest, Devarshi Steven Hartman, who model respectively the discipline and the devotion that I aspire to practice and to teach.

Special thanks to Tal Ben-Shahar, who never locked the door to his classroom and whose love of human potential ignited my own, and to all the faculty of Kripalu's Positive Psychology Program.

Thank you to all the teachers and students at Yoga to the People, my second home.

Most of all, this book is dedicated to my son, Bridge, who began becoming a person when I began writing; to our new baby, waiting to be born as I finish these words; and to my wife, Tara, whose companionship makes me a better person every day.

References

Aknin, L., C. Barrington-Leigh, E. Dunn, J. Helliwell, J. Burns, R. Biswas-Diener, and M. I. Norton. 2013. "Prosocial Spending and Well-Being." *Journal of Personality and Social Psychology* 104(4): 635–652.

Aknin, L., J. Hamlin, and E. Dunn. 2012. "Giving Leads to Happiness in Young Children." *PLoS One* 7(6): e39211.

Arnett, J. 2008. "The Neglected 95%: Why American Psychology Needs to Become Less American." *American Psychologist* 63(7): 602–614.

Baer, R. 2003. "Mindfulness Training as a Clinical Intervention: A Conceptual and Empirical Review." *Clinical Psychology: Science and Practice* 10(2): 125–143.

Baird, B., J. Smallwood, K. Mrazek, J. Kam, M. Franklin, and J. Schooler. 2012. "Inspired by Distraction: Mind Wandering Facilitates Creative Incubation." *Psychological Science* 1,117–22.

Bandura, A. 1977. "Self-efficacy: Toward a Unifying Theory of Behavioral Change." *Psychological Review* 84(2): 191–215.

Bandura, A. 1997. *Self-efficacy: The Exercise of Control*. New York: W.H. Freeman.

Bardach, A. 2012. "The Surprising—and Continuing—Influence of Swami Vivekananda." *Wall Street Journal Magazine* March 30.

Bardsley, N. 2008. "Dictator Game Giving: Altruism or Artefact?" *Experimental Economics*, 11(2): 122–133.

Bartlett, M., and D. DeSteno. 2006. "Gratitude and Prosocial Behavior Helping When It Costs You." *Psychological Science* 17(4): 319–325.

Batson, D., K. Sager, E. Garst, M. Kang, K. Rubchinsky, and K. Dawson. 1997. "Is Empathy-Induced Helping Due to Self–Other Merging?" *Journal of Personality and Social Psychology* 73(3): 495–509.

Baumeister, R. F., and J. Tierney. 2011. *Willpower: Rediscovering the Greatest Human Strength*. New York: Penguin Press.

Baumeister, R. F., E. Bratslavsky, C. Finkenauer, and K. D. Vohs. 2001. "Bad Is Stronger Than Good." *Review of General Psychology* 5(4): 323–356.

Baumeister, R. F., E. Bratslavsky, M. Muraven, and D. M. Tice. 1998. "Ego Depletion: Is The Active Self a Limited Resource?" *Journal of Personality and Social Psychology* 74(5): 1,252–1,265.

Ben-Shahar, T. 2007. *Happier*. New York: McGraw Hill.

Berkman, L. and S. Syme. 1979. "Social Networks, Host Resistance, and Mortality: A Nine-Year Follow-Up Study of Alameda County Residents." *American journal of Epidemiology* 109(2): 186–204.

Bordwell, D. 2002. "Intensified Continuity Visual Style in Contemporary American Film." *Film Quarterly* 55(3): 16–28.

Brewer, J., P. Worhunsky, J. Gray, Y. Tang, J. Weber, and H. Kober. 2011. "Meditation Experience Is Associated with Differences in Default Mode Network Activity and Connectivity." *Proceedings of the National Academy of Sciences* 108(50): 20,254–20,259.

Brickman, P., D. Coates, and R. Janoff-Bulman. 1978. "Lottery Winners and Accident Victims: Is Happiness Relative?" *Journal of Personality and Social Psychology* 36(8): 917–927.

Brown, L. 1983. "Some More Misconceptions About Psychology Among Introductory Psychology Students." *Teaching of Psychology* 10(4): 207–210.

Bushman, B. 2002. "Does Venting Anger Feed or Extinguish the Flame? Catharsis, Rumination, Distraction, Anger, and Aggressive Responding." *Personality and Social Psychology Bulletin* 28(6): 724–731.

Bushman, B., R. F. Baumeister, and A. Stack. 1999. "Catharsis, Aggression, and Persuasive Influence: Self-Fulfilling or Self-Defeating Prophecies?" *Journal of Personality and Social Psychology* 76(3): 367–376.

Bushman, B., R. F. Baumeister, and C. Phillips. 2001. "Do People Aggress to Improve Their Mood? Catharsis Beliefs, Affect Regulation Opportunity, and Aggressive Responding." *Journal of Personality and Social Psychology* 81(1): 17–32.

Campbell, J., and B. Moyers. 1991. *The Power of Myth*. New York: Random House.

Campbell, M., and F. de Waal. 2011. "Ingroup-Outgroup Bias in Contagious Yawning by Chimpanzees Supports Link to Empathy." *PLoS One*, 6(4), e18283.

Campbell, W., and C. Sedikides. 1999. "Self-Threat Magnifies the Self-Serving Bias: A Meta-Analytic Integration." *Review of General Psychology* 3(1): 23–43.

Campbell, W., C. Sedikides, G. Reeder, and A. Elliot.2000. "Among Friends? An Examination of Friendship and the Self-Serving Bias." *British Journal of Social Psychology* 39(2): 229–239.

Carlsmith, K., T. Wilson, and D. Gilbert. 2008. "The Paradoxical Consequences of Revenge." *Journal of Personality and Social Psychology* 95(6): 1,316–1,324.

Carson, J., F. Keefe, T. Lynch, K. M. Carson, V. Goli, A. M. Fras, and S. R. Thorp. 2005. "Loving-Kindness Meditation for Chronic Low Back Pain Results from a Pilot Trial." *Journal of Holistic Nursing* 23(3): 287–304.

Carter, C. 1998. "Neuroendocrine Perspectives on Social Attachment and Love." *Psychoneuroendocrinology* 23(8): 779–818.

Cialdini, R., S. Brown, B. Lewis, and S. Neuberg. 1997. "Reinterpreting the Empathy–Altruism Relationship: When One into One Equals Oneness." *Journal of Personality and Social Psychology* 73(3): 481–94.

Cope, S. 2006. *The Wisdom of Yoga*. New York: Random House.

Corfield, D., K. Murphy, and A. Guz. 1998. "Does the Motor Cortical Control of the Diaphragm 'Bypass' the Brain Stem Respiratory Centres in Man?" *Respiration Physiology* 114(2): 109–117.

Csikszentmihalyi, M. 1990. *Flow: The Psychology of Optimal Experience*. New York: HarperCollins.

Dalai Lama, H. H. 2011. *In My Own Words*. New York: Hay House.

Damasio, A. 1999. *The Feeling of What Happens*. New York: Harcourt.

Daniels, A. 2014. "As Wealthy Give Smaller Share of Income to Charity, Middle Class Digs Deeper." Retrieved from https://philanthropy.com. October 4.

Darley, J., and C. Batson. 1973. "From Jerusalem to Jericho: A Study of Situational and Dispositional Variables in Helping Behavior." *Journal of Personality and Social Psychology* 27(1): 100–108.

Davidson, R. J. 2004. "Well-being and Affective Style: Neural Substrates and Biobehavioural Correlates." *Philosophical Transactions-Royal Society of London Series B Biological Sciences* 1,395–1,412.

Davidson, R., J. Kabat-Zinn, J. Schumacher, M. Rosenkranz, D. Muller, S. Santorelli, and J. Sheridan. 2003. "Alterations in Brain and Immune Function Produced by Mindfulness Meditation." *Psychosomatic Medicine* 65(4): 564–570.

Deci, E. 1971. "Effects of Externally Mediated Rewards on Intrinsic Motivation." *Journal of Personality and Social Psychology* 18(1): 105–115.

Deci, E., and R. Ryan. 2002. *Handbook of Self-Determination Research*. Rochester: University of Rochester Press.

Deci, E., R. Koestner, and R. Ryan. 1999. "A Meta-Analytic Review of Experiments Examining the Effects of Extrinsic Rewards on Intrinsic Motivation." *Psychological Bulletin* 125(6): 627.

De Dreu, C. 2012. "Oxytocin Modulates Cooperation Within and Competition Between Groups." *Hormones and Behavior* 61(3): 419–428.

De Dreu, C., L. Greer, M. Handgraaf, S. Shalvi, G. Van Kleef, M. Baas, and S. Feith. 2010. "The Neuropeptide Oxytocin Regulates Parochial Altruism in Intergroup Conflict Among Humans." *Science* 328(5,984): 1,408–1,411.

De Mille, A. 1991. *Martha: The Life and Work of Martha Graham*. New York: Random House.

Desbordes, G., L. Negi, T. Pace, B. Wallace, C. Raison, and E. Schwartz. 2012. "Effects of Mindful-Attention and Compassion Meditation Training on Amygdala Response to Emotional Stimuli in an Ordinary, Non-Meditative State." *Frontiers in Human Neuroscience* 6: 292.

Diener, E., and M. Seligman. 2002. "Very Happy People." *Psychological Science* 13(1): 81–84.

Dietrich, A. 2003. "Functional Neuroanatomy of Altered States of Consciousness: The Transient Hypofrontality Hypothesis." *Consciousness and Cognition* 12(2): 231–256.

Dietrich, A. 2004. "Neurocognitive Mechanisms Underlying the Experience of Flow." *Consciousness and Cognition* 13(4): 746–761.

Doidge, N. 2007. *The Brain That Changes Itself*. New York: Penguin.

Duhigg, C. 2012. *The Power of Habit: Why We Do What We Do in Life and Business* (1st ed.). New York: Random House.

Duncker, K., and L. Lees. 1945. "On Problem-Solving." *Psychological Monographs* 58(5): 1–113.

Dunn, E., L. Aknin, and M. Norton. 2008. "Spending Money on Others Promotes Happiness." *Science 319* (5,870): 1,687–1,688.

Eisenberg, N., and P. Miller. 1987. "The Relation of Empathy to Prosocial and Related Behaviors." *Psychological Bulletin 101*(1): 91–119.

Eisenberg, N., R. Fabes, B. Murphy, M. Karbon, P. Maszk, M. Smith, and K. Suh. 1994. "The Relations of Emotionality and Regulation to Dispositional and Situational Empathy-Related Responding." *Journal of Personality and Social Psychology* 66(4): 776–797.

Eisenberger, N., M. Lieberman, and K. Williams. 2003. "Does Rejection Hurt? An fMRI Study of Social Exclusion." *Science 302*(5,643): 290–292.

Emmons, R. 2007. *Thanks! How Practicing Gratitude Can Make You Happier*. New York: Houghton Mifflin.

Emmons, R., and M. McCullough. 2003. "Counting Blessings versus Burdens: An Experimental Investigation of Gratitude and Subjective Well-Being in Daily Life." *Journal of Personality and Social Psychology* 84(2): 377–389.

Ewert, A. 1985. "Why People Climb: The Relationship of Participant Motives and Experience Level to Mountaineering." *Journal of Leisure Research 17*(3): 241–250.

Farb, N., Z. Segal, H. Mayberg, J. Bean, D. McKeon, Z. Fatima, and A. Anderson. 2007. "Attending to the Present: Mindfulness Meditation Reveals Distinct Neural Modes of Self-Reference." *Social Cognitive and Affective Neuroscience 2*(4): 313–322.

Farrow, T., Y. Zheng, I. Wilkinson, S. Spence, J. Deakin, N. Tarrier, and P. Woodruff. 2001. "Investigating the Functional Anatomy of Empathy and Forgiveness." *Neuroreport 12*(11): 2,433–2,438.

Feldman, G., A. Hayes, S. Kumar, J. Greeson, and J. Laurenceau. 2007. "Mindfulness and Emotion Regulation: The Development and Initial Validation of the Cognitive and Affective Mindfulness Scale-Revised." *Journal of Psychopathology and Behavioral Assessment 29*(3): 177–190.

Frankl, V. 1985. *Man's Search for Meaning*. New York: Washington Square Press.

Franklin, B. (1818) 2010. *The Autobiography of Benjamin Franklin*. New York: Tribeca Books.

Frattaroli, J. 2006. "Experimental Disclosure and Its Moderators: A Meta-Analysis." *Psychological Bulletin 132*(6): 823.

Fredrickson, B., M. Cohn, K. Coffey, J. Pek, and S. Finkel. 2008. "Open Hearts Build Lives." *Journal of Personality and Social Psychology* 95(5): 1,045–1,062.

Gandhi, M. 2010. *The Bhagavad Gita According to Gandhi*. Berkeley, CA: Berkeley Hills Books.

Gergen, K., and M. Gergen. 1988. "Narrative and the Self as Relationship." *Advances in Experimental Social Psychology* 21(1): 17–56.

Gilbert, D. 2006. *Stumbling on Happiness*. New York: Random House.

Glucksberg, S. 1962. "The Influence of Strength of Drive on Functional Fixedness and Perceptual Recognition." *Journal of Experimental Psychology* 63(1): 36–41.

Gottman, J. 1994. *What Predicts Divorce?* Florence, KY: Psychology Press.

Goyal, M., S. Singh, E. Sibinga, N. Gould, A. Rowland-Seymour, R. Sharma, and H. Shihab. 2014. "Meditation Programs for Psychological Stress and Well-Being: A Systematic Review and Meta-Analysis." *JAMA Internal Medicine* 174(3): 357–368.

Green, J., C. Sedikides, J. Saltzberg, J. Wood, and L. Forzano. 2003. "Happy Mood Decreases Self-Focused Attention." *British Journal of Social Psychology* 42(1): 147–157.

Grossman, P., L. Niemann, S. Schmidt, and H. Walach. 2004. "Mindfulness-Based Stress Reduction and Health Benefits: A Meta-Analysis." *Journal of Psychosomatic Research* 57(1): 35–43.

Gusnard, D., E. Akbudak, G. Shulman, and M. Raichle. 2001. "Medial Prefrontal Cortex and Self-Referential Mental Activity: Relation to a Default Mode of Brain Function." *Proceedings of the National Academy of Sciences* 98(7): 4,259–4,264.

Haidt, J. 2006. *The Happiness Hypothesis*. New York: Basic Books.

Hamlin, J., K. Wynn, and P. Bloom. 2010. "Three-Month-Olds Show a Negativity Bias in Their Social Evaluations." *Developmental Science* 13(6): 923–929.

Hanson, R. 2009. *Buddha's Brain: The Practical Neuroscience of Happiness, Love, and Wisdom*. Oakland, CA: New Harbinger.

Hanson, R. 2013. *Hardwiring Happiness: The New Brain Science of Contentment, Calm, and Confidence*. New York: Random House.

Harbaugh, W., U. Mayr, and D. Burghart. 2007. "Neural Responses to Taxation and Voluntary Giving Reveal Motives for Charitable Donations." *Science* 316 (5,831): 1,622–1,625.

Heine, S., and T. Hamamura. 2007. "In Search of East Asian Self-Enhancement." *Personality and Social Psychology Review* 11(1): 4–27.

Helliwell, J., and R. Putnam. 2004. "The Social Context of Well-being." *Philosophical Transactions-Royal Society of London Series B Biological Sciences* 1,435–1,446.

Henrich, J., R. Boyd, S. Bowles, C. Camerer, E. Fehr, and H. Gintis. 2004. *Foundations of Human Sociality*. New York: Oxford University Press.

Henrich, J., S. Heine, and A. Norenzayan. 2010. "The Weirdest People in the World?" *Behavioral and Brain Sciences* 33(2–3): 61–83.

Hodgins, H., and C. Knee. 2002. "The Integrating Self and Conscious Experience." *Handbook of Self-Determination Research* 87–100.

Hofmann, S., P. Grossman, and D. Hinton. 2011. "Loving-Kindness and Compassion Meditation: Potential for Psychological Interventions." *Clinical Psychology Review* 31(7): 1,126–1,132.

Hoge, E., M. Chen, E. Orr, C. Metcalf, L. Fischer, M. Pollack, N. Simon. 2013. "Loving-Kindness Meditation Practice Associated with Longer Telomeres in Women." *Brain, Behavior, and Immunity 32*: 159–163.

Holmes, T., and R. Rahe. 1967. "The Social Readjustment Rating Scale." *Journal of Psychosomatic Research 11*(2): 213–218.

Holt-Lunstad, J., T. Smith, T., and J. Layton. 2010. "Social Relationships and Mortality Risk: A Meta-Analytic Review." *PLoS Medicine 7*(7): e1000316.

Huber, D., P. Veinante, and R. Stoop. 2005. "Vasopressin and Oxytocin Excite Distinct Neuronal Populations in the Central Amygdala." *Science 308*(5,719): 245–248.

Hutcherson, C., E. Seppala, and J. Gross. 2008. "Loving-Kindness Meditation Increases Social Connectedness." *Emotion 8*(5): 720–724.

Jacobs, T., E. Epel, J. Lin, E. Blackburn, O. Wolkowitz, D. Bridwell, and K. MacLean. 2011. "Intensive Meditation Training, Immune Cell Telomerase Activity, and Psychological Mediators." *Psychoneuroendocrinology 36*(5): 664–681.

James, W. 1890. *The Principles of Psychology.* New York: Henry Holt and Company.

James, W. 1914. *Habit.* New York: Henry Holt and Company.

James, W. 1985. *The Varieties of Religious Experience.* Cambridge, MA: Harvard University Press.

Jazaieri, H., G. Jinpa, K. McGonigal, E. Rosenberg, J. Finkelstein, E. Simon-Thomas, and P. Goldin. 2013. "Enhancing Compassion: A Randomized Controlled Trial of a Compassion Cultivation Training Program." *Journal of Happiness Studies 14*(4): 1,113–1,126.

Kabat-Zinn, J. 2012. *Mindfulness for Beginners.* Boulder, CO: Sounds True.

Kafka, F. 2012. *A Hunger Artist and Other Stories.* New York: Oxford University Press.

Kahneman, D., and A. Deaton. 2010. "High Income Improves Evaluation of Life but Not Emotional Well-being." *Proceedings of the National Academy of Sciences 107*(38): 16,489–16,493.

Kahneman, D., and A. Tversky. 1979. "Prospect Theory: An Analysis of Decision Under Risk." *Econometrica: Journal of the Econometric Society* 263–291.

Kahneman, D., and A. Tversky. 1984. "Choices, Values, and Frames." *American Psychologist 39*(4): 341–350.

Kahneman, D., A. Krueger, D. Schkade, N. Schwarz, and A. Stone. 2006. "Would You Be Happier if You Were Richer? A Focusing Illusion." *Science 312* (5,782): 1,908–1910.

Kasser, T., and R. Ryan. 1996. "Further Examining the American Dream: Differential Correlates of Intrinsic and Extrinsic Goals." *Personality and Social Psychology Bulletin 22*: 280–287.

Keng, S., M. Smoski, and C. Robins. 2011. "Effects of Mindfulness on Psychological Health: A Review of Empirical Studies." *Clinical psychology review 31*(6): 1,041–1,056.

Khoury, B., T. Lecomte, G. Fortin, M. Masse, P. Therien, V. Bouchard, and S. Hofmann. 2013. "Mindfulness-Based Therapy: A Comprehensive Meta-Analysis. *Clinical Psychology Review* 33(6): 763–771.

Killingsworth, M., and D. Gilbert. 2010. "A Wandering Mind Is An Unhappy Mind." *Science* 330(6,006): 932.

Kirsch, P., C. Esslinger, Q. Chen, D. Mier, S. Lis, S. Siddhanti, and A. Meyer-Lindenberg. 2005. "Oxytocin Modulates Neural Circuitry for Social Cognition and Fear in Humans." *The Journal of Neuroscience* 25(49): 11,489–11,493.

Kosfeld, M., M. Heinrichs, P. Zak, U. Fischbacher, and E. Fehr. 2005. "Oxytocin Increases Trust in Humans." *Nature* 435(7,042): 673–676.

Kraut, R., M. Patterson, V. Lundmark, S. Kiesler, T. Mukophadhyay, and W. Scherlis. 1998. "Internet Paradox: A Social Technology That Reduces Social Involvement and Psychological Well-Being?" *American Psychologist* 53(9): 1,017–1,031.

Krebs, D. 1975. "Empathy and Altruism." *Journal of Personality and Social Psychology* 32(6): 1,134–1,146.

Kross, E., P. Verduyn, E. Demiralp, J. Park, D. S. Lee, N. Lin, and O. Ybarra. 2013. "Facebook Use Predicts Declines in Subjective Well-Being in Young Adults." *PLoS One* 8(8): e69841.

Krueger, A., and D. Schkade. 2008. "The Reliability of Subjective Well-Being Measures." *Journal of public economics* 92(8): 1,833–1,845.

Kruger, J., and D. Dunning. 1999. "Unskilled and Unaware of It: How Difficulties in Recognizing One's Own Incompetence Lead to Inflated Self-Assessments." *Journal of Personality and Social Psychology* 77(6): 1,121–1,134.

Lawler, K., J. Younger, R. L. Piferi, R. L. Jobe, K. A. Edmondson, and W. Jones. 2005. "The Unique Effects of Forgiveness on Health: An Exploration of Pathways." *Journal of Behavioral Medicine* 28(2): 157–167.

Leary, M., E. Tate, C. Adams, A. Batts Allen, and J. Hancock. 2007. "Self-Compassion and Reactions to Unpleasant Self-Relevant Events: The Implications of Treating Oneself Kindly." *Journal of Personality and Social Psychology* 92(5): 887–904.

Lepper, M., G. Sagotsky, J. Dafoe, and D. Greene. 1982. "Consequences of Superfluous Social Constraints: Effects on Young Children's Social Inferences and Subsequent Intrinsic Interest." *Journal of Personality and Social Psychology* 42(1): 51–65.

Levenson, R., P. Ekman, and M. Ricard. 2012. "Meditation and the Startle Response: A Case Study." *Emotion* 12(3): 650–658.

Linley, P., K. Nielsen, R. Gillett, and R. Biswas-Diener. 2010. "Using Signature Strengths in Pursuit of Goals." *International Coaching Psychology Review* 5(1): 6–15.

List, J. 2007. "On the Interpretation of Giving in Dictator Games." *Journal of Political Economy* 115(3): 482–493.

Locke, E., and G. Latham. 2002. "Building a Practically Useful Theory of Goal Setting and Task Motivation: A 35-Year Odyssey." *American Psychologist* 57(9): 705–717.

Luskin, F. 2002. *Forgive for Good*. New York: HarperCollins.

Lutz, A., J. Brefczynski-Lewis, T. Johnstone, and R. Davidson. 2008. "Regulation of the Neural Circuitry of Emotion by Compassion Meditation." *PLoS One* 3(3): e1897.

Lutz, A., H. Slagter, J. Dunne, and R. Davidson. 2008. "Attention Regulation and Monitoring in Meditation." *Trends in Cognitive Sciences* 12(4): 163–169.

Lutz, A., L. Greischar, N. Rawlings, M. Ricard, and R. Davidson. 2004. "Long-Term Meditators Self-Induce High-Amplitude Gamma Synchrony During Mental Practice." *Proceedings of the National Academy of Sciences of the United States of America* 101(46): 16,369–16,373.

Lyubomirsky, S., and H. Lepper. 1999. "A Measure of Subjective Happiness: Preliminary Reliability and Construct Validation." *Social Indicators Research* 46(2): 137–155.

Lyubomirsky, S., C. Tkach, and K. Sheldon. 2004. "Pursuing Sustained Happiness Through Random Acts of Kindness and Counting One's Blessings: Tests of Two Six-Week Interventions." *Unpublished raw data*.

Lyubomirsky, S., K. Sheldon, and D. Schkade. 2005. "Pursuing Happiness: The Architecture of Sustainable Change." *Review of General Psychology* 9(2) 111–131.

Lyubomirsky, S., L. King, and E. Diener. 2005. "The Benefits of Frequent Positive Affect: Does Happiness Lead to Success?" *Psychological Bulletin*, 131(6): 803–855.

Lyubomirsky, S., L. Sousa, and R. Dickerhoof. 2006. "The Costs and Benefits of Writing, Talking, and Thinking about Life's Triumphs and Defeats." *Journal of Personality and Social Psychology* 90(4): 692–708.

Mark, G., D. Gudith, and U. Klocke. 2008. *The Cost of Interrupted Work: More Speed and Stress*. Paper presented at the Proceedings of the SIGCHI conference on Human Factors in Computing Systems.

Maslach, C. 2003. *Burnout: The Cost of Caring*. Cambridge, MA: Malor Books.

Maslach, C., W. Schaufeli, and M. Leiter. 2001. "Job Burnout." *Annual Review of Psychology* 52(1): 397–422.

Maslow, A. 1943. "A Theory of Human Motivation." *Psychological Review* 50(4): 370–96.

Maslow, A. 1964. *Religions, Values & Peak Experiences*. Columbus, OH: Ohio State University Press.

Mason, M., M. Norton, J. Van Horn, D. Wegner, S. Grafton, and C. Macrae. 2007. "Wandering Minds: The Default Network and Stimulus-Independent Thought." *Science* 315(5,810): 393–395.

McCall, C., N. Steinbeis, M. Ricard, and T. Singer. 2014. "Compassion Meditators Show Less Anger, Less Punishment, and More Compensation of Victims in Response to Fairness Violations." *Frontiers in Behavioral Neuroscience* 8: 424.

McCullough, M., K. Pargament, and C. Thoresen. 2001. *Forgiveness: Theory, Research, and Practice*. New York: Guilford.

McPherson, M., L. Smith-Lovin, and M. Brashears. 2006. "Social Isolation in America: Changes in Core Discussion Networks over Two Decades." *American Sociological Review 71*(3): 353–375.

Mezulis, A., L. Abramson, J. Hyde, and B. Hankin. 2004. "Is There a Universal Positivity Bias in Attributions? A Meta-Analytic Review." *Psychological Bulletin 130*(5): 711–747.

Mor, N., and J. Winquist. 2002. "Self-Focused Attention and Negative Affect: A Meta-Analysis." *Psychological Bulletin 128*(4): 638–662.

Nakamura, J., and M. Csikszentmihalyi. 2002. "The Concept of Flow." *Handbook of Positive Psychology* 89–105.

Nakamura, J., and M. Csikszentmihalyi. 2009. "Flow Theory and Research." In *Oxford Handbook of Positive Psychology*, ed. S. Lopez and C. Snyder. New York: Oxford University Press.

Neff, K., and C. Germer. 2013. A Pilot Study and Randomized Controlled Trial of the Mindful Self-Compassion Program. *Journal of Clinical Psychology 69*(1): 2844.

Neff, K., S. Rude, and K. Kirkpatrick. 2007. "An Examination of Self-Compassion in Relation to Positive Psychological Functioning and Personality Traits." *Journal of Research in Personality 41*(4): 908–916.

Norcross, J., M. Mrykalo, and M. Blagys. 2002. "Auld Lang Syne: Success Predictors, Change Processes, and Self-Reported Outcomes of New Year's Resolvers and Nonresolvers." *Journal of Clinical Psychology 58*(4): 397–405.

Nørretranders, T. 1998. *The User Illusion*, translated by J. Sydenham. New York: Viking.

Nozick, R. 1974. *Anarchy, State, and Utopia*. New York: Basic Books.

Olds, J., and P. Milner. 1954. "Positive Reinforcement Produced by Electrical Stimulation of Septal Area and Other Regions of Rat Brain." *Journal of Comparative and Physiological Psychology 47*(6): 419–427.

O'Leary, A. 1992. "Self-efficacy and Health: Behavioral and Stress-Physiological Mediation." *Cognitive Therapy and Research 16*(2): 229–245.

Ophir, E., C. Nass, and A. Wagner. 2009. "Cognitive Control in Media Multitaskers." *Proceedings of the National Academy of Sciences 106*(37): 15,583–15,587.

Pace, T., L. Negi, D. Adame, S. Cole, T. Sivilli, T. Brown, and C. Raison. 2009. "Effect of Compassion Meditation on Neuroendocrine, Innate Immune and Behavioral Responses to Psychosocial Stress." *Psychoneuroendocrinology 34*(1): 87–98.

Parkes, M. 2006. "Breath-Holding and Its Breakpoint." *Experimental Physiology 91*(1): 1–15.

Peifer, C. 2012. "Psychophysiological Correlates of Flow-Experience." *Advances in Flow Research* 139–164.

Pennebaker, J. 1997. "Writing about Emotional Experiences as a Therapeutic Process." *Psychological Science 8*(3): 162–166.

Pennebaker, J., and J. Seagal, J. 1999. "Forming a Story: The Health Benefits of Narrative." *Journal of Clinical Psychology 55*(10) 1,243–1,254.

Piff, P., M. Kraus, S. Côté, B. Cheng, and D. Keltner. 2010. "Having Less, Giving More: The Influence of Social Class on Prosocial Behavior." *Journal of Personality and Social Psychology* 99(5): 771–784.

Piff, P., D. Stancato, S. Côté, R. Mendoza-Denton, and D. Keltner. 2012. "Higher Social Class Predicts Increased Unethical Behavior." *Proceedings of the National Academy of Sciences* 109(11): 4,086–4,091.

Piliavin, J., and E. Siegl. 2007. "Health Benefits of Volunteering in the Wisconsin Longitudinal Study." *Journal of Health and Social Behavior* 48(4): 450–464.

Pink, D. 2009. *Drive: The Surprising Truth about What Motivates Us.* New York: Riverhead Books.

Pronin, E., and M. Kugler. 2007. "Valuing Thoughts, Ignoring Behavior: The Introspection Illusion as a Source of the Bias Blind Spot." *Journal of Experimental Social Psychology* 43(4): 565–578.

Proust, M. 1922. *Swann's Way.* Trans. C. Scott-Moncrieff. New York: Holt.

Putnam, R. 1995. "Bowling Alone: America's Declining Social Capital." *Journal of Democracy* 6(1): 65–78.

Rand, D., J. Greene, and M. Nowak. 2012. "Spontaneous Giving and Calculated Greed." *Nature* 489 (7,416): 427–430.

Reb, J., S. Junjie, and J. Narayanan. 2010. *Compassionate Dictators? The Effects of Loving-kindness Meditation on Offers in a Dictator Game.* Paper presented at the The Effects of Loving-Kindness Meditation on Offers in a Dictator Game. IACM 23rd Annual Conference Paper.

Redelmeier, D., J. Katz, and D. Kahneman. 2003. "Memories of Colonoscopy." *Pain* 104(1): 187–194.

Reker, G., E. Peacock, and P. Wong. 1987. "Meaning and Purpose in Life and Well-Being: A Life-Span Perspective." *Journal of Gerontology* 42(1): 44–49.

Roese, N., and J. Olson. 2014. *What Might Have Been: The Social Psychology of Counterfactual Thinking.* New York: Psychology Press.

Rubinstein, J., Meyer, D., and Evans, J. 2001. "Executive Control of Cognitive Processes in Task Switching." *Journal of Experimental Psychology* 27(4): 763–797.

Sadato, N., A. Pascual-Leone, J. Grafman, M. Deiber, V. Ibanez, and M. Hallett. 1998. "Neural Networks for Braille Reading by the Blind." *Brain* 121(7): 1,213–1,229.

Sargeant, W. 2009. *The Bhagavad Gita.* Albany: State University of New York.

Schkade, D., and D. Kahneman. 1998. "Does Living in California Make People Happy?" *Psychological Science* 9(5): 340–346.

Schooler, J., D. Ariely, and G. Loewenstein. 2003. "The Pursuit of Happiness Can Be Self-Defeating." In *The Psychology of Economic Decisions*, ed. J. Carillo. Oxford: Oxford University Press.

Schutte, N., and J. Malouff. 2014. "A Meta-Analytic Review of the Effects of Mindfulness Meditation on Telomerase Activity. *Psychoneuroendocrinology* 42, 45–48.

Sedikides, C., W. Campbell, G. Reeder, and A. Elliot. 1998. "The Self-Serving Bias in Relational Context." *Journal of Personality and Social Psychology* 74(2): 378–386.

Seligman, M. 2002. *Authentic Happiness.* New York: Simon & Schuster.

Seligman, M., and C. Peterson. 2004. *Character Strengths and Virtues.* Washington, DC: APA Press.

Dr. Seuss. (1961) 2006. *The Sneetches and Other Stories.* HarperCollins UK.

Sheldon, K., and A. Elliot. 1999. "Goal Striving, Need Satisfaction, and Longitudinal Well-Being." *Journal of Personality and Social Psychology* 76(3): 482–497.

Shirtcliff, E., M. Vitacco, A. Graf, A. Gostisha, J. Merz, and C. Zahn-Waxler. 2009. "Neurobiology of Empathy and Callousness." *Behavioral Sciences and the Law* 27(2): 137–171.

Simons, D., and C. Chabris. 2011. "What People Believe about How Memory Works." *PLoS One* 6(8): e22757.

Singer, T., and M. Bolz. 2013. *Compassion: Bridging Practice and Science.* Munich: Max Planck Society.

Smallwood, J., and J. Andrews-Hanna. 2013. "Not All Minds That Wander Are Lost: The Importance of a Balanced Perspective on the Mind-Wandering State." *Frontiers in Psychology* 4: 441.

Smyth, J. 1998. "Written Emotional Expression: Effect Sizes, Outcome Types, and Moderating Variables." *Journal of Consulting and Clinical Psychology* 66(1): 174–184.

Stern, K. 2013. "Why the Rich Don't Give to Charity." *Atlantic.* March 20.

Stevens, W. 1957. *Opus Posthumous.* New York: Knopf.

Stone, M. 2008. *The Inner Tradition of Yoga.* Boston: Shambhala.

Tajfel, H. 2010. *Social Identity and Intergroup Relations.* New York: Cambridge University Press.

Tajfel, H., M. Billig, R. Bundy, and C. Flament. 1971. "Social Categorization and Intergroup Behaviour." *European Journal of Social Psychology* 1(2): 149–178.

Tang, Y., Y. Ma, J. Wang, Y. Fan, S. Feng, Q. Lu, and M. Fan. 2007. "Short-term Meditation Training Improves Attention and Self-regulation." *Proceedings of the National Academy of Sciences* 104(43): 17,152–17,156.

Taylor, S., L. Klein, B. Lewis, T. Gruenewald, R. Gurung, and J. Updegraff. 2000. "Biobehavioral Responses to Stress in Females: Tend-and-Befriend, Not Fight-or-Flight." *Psychological Review* 107(3): 411–429.

Thoits, P., and L. Hewitt. 2001. "Volunteer Work and Well-being." *Journal of Health and Social Behavior* 115–131.

Toussaint, L., and D. Williams. 2003. *Physiological Correlates of Forgiveness.* Paper presented at A Campaign for Forgiveness Research Conference, Atlanta, GA.

Toussaint, L., D. Williams, M. Musick, and S. Everson. 2001. "Forgiveness and Health: Age Differences in a U.S. Probability Sample." *Journal of Adult Development* 8(4): 249–257.

Valdesolo, P., and D. DeSteno. 2011. "Synchrony and the Social Tuning of Compassion." *Emotion* 11(2): 262–266.

Warneken, F., and M. Tomasello. 2006. "Altruistic Helping in Human Infants and Young Chimpanzees." *Science* 311(5,765): 1,301–1,303.

Weng, H., A. Fox, A. Shackman, D. Stodola, J. Caldwell, M. Olson, and R. Davidson. 2013. "Compassion Training Alters Altruism and Neural Responses to Suffering." *Psychological Science* 24(7): 1,171–1,180.

White, R. 1959. "Motivation Reconsidered: The Concept of Competence." *Psychological Review* 66(5): 297–333.

Wiese, B., and A. Freund. 2005. "Goal Progress Makes One Happy, or Does It? Longitudinal Findings from the Work Domain." *Journal of Occupational and Organizational Psychology* 78(2): 287–304.

Wilson, T. 2002. *Strangers to Ourselves.* Cambridge: Harvard University Press.

Wilson, T., and D. Gilbert. 2003. "Affective Forecasting." *Advances in Experimental Social Psychology* 35: 345–411.

Wilson, T., D. Gilbert, and D. Centerbar. 2003. "Making Sense: The Causes of Emotional Evanescence." *The Psychology of Economic Decisions* 1: 209–233.

Wilson, T., D. Reinhard, E. Westgate, D. Gilbert, N. Ellerbeck, C. Hahn, and A. Shaked. 2014. "Just Think: The Challenges of the Disengaged Mind." *Science* 345(6,192): 75–77.

Winfrey, O. 2000. *What I Know for Sure.* New York: O, The Oprah Magazine.

Witvliet, C. V., T. Ludwig, and K. Vander Laan. 2001. "Granting Forgiveness or Harboring Grudges." *Psychological Science* 12(2): 117–123.

Wood, A., P. Linley, J. Maltby, T. Kashdan, and R. Hurling. 2011. "Using Personal and Psychological Strengths Leads to Increases in Well-Being over Time." *Personality and Individual Differences* 50(1): 15–19.

Wood, J., J. Saltzberg, and L. Goldsamt. 1990. "Does Affect Induce Self-Focused Attention?" *Journal of Personality and Social Psychology* 58(5): 899–908.

Worthington, E. 2008. *Steps to REACH Forgiveness and to Reconcile.* Upper Saddle River, NJ: Pearson Learning Solutions.

Wrosch, C., I. Bauer, and M. Scheier. 2005. "Regret and Quality of Life Across the Adult Life Span: The Influence of Disengagement and Available Future Goals." *Psychology and Aging* 20(4): 657–670.

Wrosch, C., I. Bauer, G. Miller, and S. Lupien. 2007. "Regret Intensity, Diurnal Cortisol Secretion, and Physical Health in Older Individuals." *Psychology and Aging* 22(2): 319–330.

Xu, X., X. Zuo, X. Wang, and S. Han. 2009. "Do You Feel My Pain? Racial Group Membership Modulates Empathic Neural Responses." *The Journal of Neuroscience* 29(26): 8,525–8,529.

Zak, P., A. Stanton, and S. Ahmadi. 2007. "Oxytocin Increases Generosity in Humans." *PLoS One* 2(11): e1128.

Zika, S., and K. Chamberlain. 1992. "On the Relation Between Meaning in Life and Psychological Well-Being." *British Journal of Psychology* 83(1): 133–145.

Sam Chase is co-owner of a Yoga to the People studio in New York City, where he leads weekly yoga programs for everyday people and diverse organizations, including New York University and the United Nations. He received his master's degree at Harvard's A.R.T. Institute, and certificates in yoga and positive psychology from the Kripalu Center. Chase resides in Brooklyn, NY.

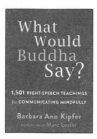
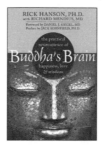

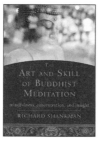